A Study on Consumers Attitude, Preference & Buying Practices towards Green Products in Coimbatore City

Dr.B. Devipriya

Dr.M. Nandhini

Published by

BONFRING®
Intellectual Integrity

ISBN 978-93-86638-34-2

Authors

Dr.B. Devipriya
Dr.M. Nandhini

Bonfring

309, 2nd Floor, 5th Street Extension, Gandhipuram,
Coimbatore-641 012.
Tamilnadu, India.
E-mail: info@bonfring.org | Website: www.bonfring.org
Phone: 0422 4213231

<table>
<thead>
<tr><th>Chapter</th><th>Contents</th><th>Page No</th></tr>
</thead>
<tbody>
<tr><td>I</td><td>Introduction and Research Design</td><td>1</td></tr>
<tr><td></td><td>1.1. Introduction</td><td>1</td></tr>
<tr><td></td><td>1.2. Significance of the Study</td><td>2</td></tr>
<tr><td></td><td>1.3. Statement of the Problem</td><td>3</td></tr>
<tr><td></td><td>1.4. Conceptual Framework of the Study</td><td>4</td></tr>
<tr><td></td><td>1.5. Scope of the Study</td><td>5</td></tr>
<tr><td></td><td>1.6. Objectives of the Study</td><td>5</td></tr>
<tr><td></td><td>1.7. Hypotheses of the Study</td><td>5</td></tr>
<tr><td></td><td>1.8. Research Methodology</td><td>6</td></tr>
<tr><td></td><td>1.8.1. Study Area</td><td>7</td></tr>
<tr><td></td><td>1.8.2. Sampling Framework</td><td>7</td></tr>
<tr><td></td><td>1.8.3. Sample Size Justification</td><td>7</td></tr>
<tr><td></td><td>1.8.4. Sources of Data</td><td>8</td></tr>
<tr><td></td><td>1.8.5. Data Reliability and Validity</td><td>8</td></tr>
<tr><td></td><td>1.9. Operational Concept</td><td>9</td></tr>
<tr><td></td><td>1.10. Statistical Tools Applied</td><td>11</td></tr>
<tr><td></td><td>1.11. Limitations of the Study</td><td>12</td></tr>
<tr><td></td><td>1.12. Chapter Organisation Scheme</td><td>13</td></tr>
<tr><td>II</td><td>Review of Literature</td><td>14</td></tr>
<tr><td></td><td>2.1. Introduction</td><td>14</td></tr>
<tr><td></td><td>2.2. Green Products</td><td>14</td></tr>
<tr><td></td><td>2.3. Understanding the Concept of Green Marketing and its Definitions</td><td>16</td></tr>
<tr><td></td><td>2.4. Role of Marketers in Selling Green Products</td><td>19</td></tr>
<tr><td></td><td>2.5. Consumers' Awareness and Attitude towards Green Marketing and Products</td><td>21</td></tr>
<tr><td></td><td>2.6. Consumers' Perception and Buying Behaviour towards Green Marketing</td><td>23</td></tr>
<tr><td></td><td>2.7. Challenges and Opportunities of Green Products</td><td>27</td></tr>
</tbody>
</table>

Marketing

2.8. Conclusion–Research Gap   29

III   Overview on Green Marketing: Consumers Attitude and Preferences towards Green Products   30

3.1. Evolution of Green Marketing Concept   30

3.2. United Nations Environment Programme on Environment Protection   31

    3.2.1. United Nations Environment Programme   32

    3.2.2. The United Nations Framework Convention on Climate Change   33

3.3. Need of Green Marketing   35

3.4. Green Marketing Concept   36

3.5. Concept of Green Marketing in Asia   37

3.6. Green Consciousness among Indians in Traditional and Middle Era   38

3.7. Green Marketing in India in Modern Era   40

3.8. Main Reasons for Adopting the Concept of Green Marketing by Indian Firms   41

    3.8.1. Governmental Pressure   41

    3.8.2. Corporate Social Responsibility and Green Marketing   42

3.9. Marketing Mix of Green Marketing   42

    3.9.1. Green Products and Its Characteristics   45

    3.9.2. Nature of Green Products   46

    3.9.3. Promotional Strategies for Green Products   48

3.10. Understanding Green Consumers   49

3.11. Challenges of Green Marketing   49

3.12. Success of Green Marketing   52

3.13. Reasons for Companies Going Green   53

3.14. Conclusion   54

References   54

IV	**Analysis and Interpretation**	**62**
	4.1. Introduction	62
	4.1.1. Demographic and Socio-economic Status of the Consumers	62
	4.1.2. Consumers' Awareness about Green Products	66
	4.1.3. Consumers' Attitude towards Green Products	72
	4.1.4. Green Products Buying Behaviour among Consumers	79
	4.1.5. Consumers Level of Perception and Satisfaction towards Green Products	88
	4.1.6. Consumers' Belief on Benefits of Buying Green Products	105
	4.1.7. Problems Faced by the Consumers' of Green Products	128
	4.1.8. Consumers' Intention Towards Future Buying of Green Products	131
	4.1.9. Structural Equation Model	138
	4.2. Conclusion	141
V	**Summary, Findings, Suggestions, Conclusion and Scope for Further Research**	**144**
	5.1. Summary of the Study	144
	5.2. Findings of the Study	145
	5.2.1. Demographic and Socio-Economic Status of the Consumers	145
	5.2.2. Consumers' Awareness about Green Products	145
	5.2.3. Consumers' Attitude towards Green Products	146
	5.2.4. Consumers Buying Behaviour towards Green Products	146
	5.2.5. Consumers Level of Perception and Satisfaction towards Green Products	146
	5.2.6. Consumers' Belief on Benefits of Buying Green Products	147

5.2.7. Problems Faced by the Consumers' while Buying Green Products   147

5.2.8. Consumers' Intention towards Future Buying of Green products   147

5.3. Suggestions   148

5.3.1. Increasing Awareness on Green Products   148

5.3.2. Exhibiting Fair and Genuine Marketing Practices   148

5.3.3. Increase the Frequency of Buying Green Products   149

5.3.4. Adhering to Innovation and Modernisation in Green Products   149

5.3.5. Focus on More Promotions and Offers   150

5.3.6. Pay Attention to the Product Package and Labelling   150

5.4. Conclusion   150

5.5. Future Scope of the Study   151

References   151

CHAPTER I

INTRODUCTION AND RESEARCH DESIGN

1.1. Introduction

"Green" is the word of the day and "Green Marketing" and "Green Products" are future of today's manufacturers and marketers. Rapidly changing environment is now a major concern for the people throughout world, making them more and more concerned about the environment. Today people are beginning to realise their role and responsibilities towards the environment. To have a sustainable, pollution-free environment, it is paramount to implement the concept of green marketing, so that people are educated in this regard as much as possible. Although this change is not happening quickly, it is happening in a slow phase. Modern day business enterprises are looking towards gaining an edge in the green market industry by introducing innovative green products that are more environment-friendly. They are cutting down on extras and wasted materials and turning their operations into more efficient and green operation. Green product manufacturers have also started to educate the masses with an increase in advertising that puts emphasis on green products and how they are more beneficial for the consumers.

Green marketing thrives on the underlying philosophy 'Reduce, Reuse and Recycle'. Green or Environmental Marketing consists of all activities designed to generate and facilitate any exchanges intended to satisfy human needs or wants, such that the satisfaction of these needs and wants occurs, with minimal detrimental impact on the natural environment. It ensures that the interests of the organisation and all its consumers are protected, as voluntary exchange will not take place unless both the buyer and seller mutually benefit.

The business on green products such as environmental friendly personal care products have started to grow in the consumer market. It is also said that green marketing incorporates a broad range of activities, including product modification, changes to the production process, packaging changes, as well as modifying advertising. In short, defining green marketing is not a simple task where several meanings intersect and contradict with each other.

From the above discussion it can be concluded that green marketing is considered as one of the major trends in modern businesses. Consumers are therefore, becoming more sensitive in their environmental attitudes, preferences and purchases. The desire of consumers to purchase green products and services is rising. Many are more aware of environmental issues and consequently choose products that do not damage the environment over less environmentally friendly products, even if they cost more. Environmentally preferable products are sometimes more expensive to purchase than other alternative products. Moreover, green consumers are willing to pay a higher price for environmentally friendly products, which is a huge opportunity for companies as well as governments looking to make green policy changes. Thus, the increasing numbers of consumers who prefer and are willing to buy eco-friendly products are creating opportunity for business, that are selling "Green" or "environmentally friendly products" as a component of their value proposition. Businesses that offer products which are manufactured and designed with an environmental marketing mix have a long-term competitive advantage. A better understanding of consumers' buying behaviour will allow businesses to acquire more market-applicable approach to sustain in the competitive market.

The marketers should realise the fact that consumers' buying behaviour has a strong influence in terms of their purchases. Green marketers not only trigger the consumer purchasing process but, it also influences consumers' perception towards a product. This complicated process enables businesses to attract new consumers and adapt their products or services according to their needs and wants or as per changing consumers' behaviour towards their products or services. Consumers tend to reduce the impact of harmful chemicals and products on the environment through their sensible purchasing decisions. Based on the above discussion a rational idea has been generated to analyse the consumers' attitude, preferences and buying practices towards green products. Thus, this study aims to analyse consumers' attitude, preferences and buying practices towards green products. This study is focused on the green consumers living in the Coimbatore City of Tamil Nadu.

1.2. Significance of the Study

With the threat of global warming looming large, it is extremely important that green marketing becomes the norm rather than an exception or just a fad. Green marketing assumes even more importance and relevance in developing countries like India. The environmental problems in India are growing rapidly. Way back in 1991, the Government recognised the need for increased consumer awareness on eco-friendly (or green) products and launched the eco-labelling scheme known as `Ecomark'. This scheme aimed to have a mechanism for easy identification of environment-friendly products. However, the scheme did not succeed. Over the years there are some internationally accepted eco-labels which are available in India. Most of the green products manufacturers have applied these schemes to get an easy access to the developed markets. The Indian domestic market for green products has over the years been driven by green claims made by the manufactures with little or no evidence to back up their claims. The Indian consumers, particularly the middle-class consumers, over the last two decades have become environmentally more conscious. The 2012 Greendex survey reflected, that though Indian consumers prefer choosing to buy environmentally friendly products, a high percentage of consumers are sceptical of green products i.e., they are doubtful about the authencity of the products. At this juncture changing consumer attitude towards green products raises the need for the various green products manufacturers and marketers to move away from their business of usual products and to sell more green products in Indian markets. Surely, there is distinct interest amongst the consumers to buy green products. Based on the above discussion it is imperative to assess the perception of the customers on the environmental attributes of products as well as to understand the barriers perceived in acceptance of green products.

1.3. Statement of the Problem

Modern day consumers are more sensitive to environmental an issue, which is well reflected in their attitude, preferences for green products and even their buying behaviour replicate their intention. Increasing number of consumers who prefer and willing to buy green products are creating opportunities for businesses for manufacturing and sales of green products. In fact, it is a well-recognised fact that businesses that offer products that are manufactured and designed with an environmental marketing mix have a long-term competitive advantage in comparison to the sales of non-green products. Modern day consumers greatly value the direct benefits that green products offer, such as superior freshness and taste, the promise of safety and health, and savings on energy costs. Consumers are attracted to green products because they leave a smaller carbon footprint, leaving pollution-free green environment. The manufacturers and marketers of green products have to realise the fact that consumers prefer products that do not harm the natural environment as also the human health. If consumers are becoming more concerned about their everyday habits, it will in turn impact on the environment. Outcome of this behaviour will reflect in the translation of consumers' attitude and preferences for buying green products and avoid buying of chemical-based non-organic products. In short it can be said that consumers are becoming more and more committed to buy green products. Drawing a detailed understanding from the above discussion a curiosity has been raised to draw a micro level analysis on the consumers' attitude, preferences and buying practices towards green products. This study is focused on the green consumers from Coimbatore city in Tamil Nadu.

1.4. Conceptual Framework of the Study

The concept of environmentally friendly or Green products is not new. Since ages, the conservation ethics have been an inseparable part of Indian thought, traditions and day-to-day consumption. But, since the independence of the nation in 1947, the white, green and industrial revolution had moved the manufacturers and consumers towards utilisation and consumption of non-organic products or those products that are manufactured with chemical base. The pro-environmental activities started in the last 1980 are focused on environmental protection. Pro-environmental concern is conceptualised as a general attitude that reflects the extent to which the consumer is worried about the threats to the environment and green consumers who would be willing to pay premium prices for more environmentally friendly products. With green marketing, advertisers, the various consumer product manufacturers and marketers have started their focus on selling environmental benefits products such as biodegradable, energy-efficient, environmentally safe and recyclable.

Green products or the concept of green marketing covers the overall brand of marketing activities undertaken by companies in a manner that they promote manufacture of products which have a positive impact on environment or alternatively reduce negative impact on the environment. There have been a number of different factors which are instrumental in promoting green consumers to purchase green products. Extensive research over the years identify that heightened awareness of green issues; increased level of information availability on environmental sustenance; green advertising by corporations; increased concern for the environment; increase in popularity of green products by social and environmental charity organisations have changed the consumers' attitude and preferences for green products. These discussions have provided required scope for framing the concept and conduct of this study. This study aims to analyse the consumers' attitude, preferences and buying behaviour towards green products.

The potential for the growth of green products is more in India. To harshness the full opportunity the manufacturers and marketers of various consumers' products have to concentrate on the concept of producing those products that could support in protection of environment and provide remedial measures for environmental problems. For this to happen in a successful manner there is a need for developing innovative integration of green products with other non-conventional products, developing new marketing technologies, initiating new process and communicating the same to the potential and existing customers. As an initial step to these activities, this study aims to assess consumers' attitude, preferences and buying practices towards green products in Coimbatore City, Tamil Nadu.

1.5. Scope of the Study

It is strongly believed that the findings of this study will help the manufacturers, marketers of green products and research scholars in drawing required first-hand knowledge on consumers' attitude, preferences and buying behaviour towards green products in the study region i.e., Coimbatore city. The study can support them in understanding the need for developing innovative integration of green products with other non-conventional products, developing new marketing technologies, initiating new process and communicating the same to the potential and existing customers.

1.6. Objectives of the Study

Based on the identified scope of the study the following objectives are framed:

- To study the demographic and socio-economic status of green product consumers living in Coimbatore city.
- To analyse the consumers' awareness and attitude towards green products available in the market.
- To critically evaluate the green products buying behaviour among consumers.
- To measure the consumers' perception and satisfaction towards green products available in the market.
- To measure the prevailing gap in the consumers' perception and satisfaction towards green products available in the market and to evaluate their future buying intention of green products.

1.7. Hypotheses of the Study

To draw empirical justification to the objectives of the study following hypotheses are framed and tested.

- There exists a close association between consumers' level of awareness towards green products and their demographic and socio-economic status.
- Consumers' level of awareness towards green products does not support them in recognising products as green or not.
- Consumers' level of awareness towards green products greatly influences their level of attitude towards it.
- The factors that influence consumers for buying green products do not differ from one individual to another.

- Consumers' level of attitude towards green products greatly influences their level of perceptions towards it.
- There exists a close association between consumers' level of perception towards green products and level of satisfaction towards it.
- Consumers' level of agreeability about benefits obtained by buying green products varies among their demographic and socio–economic status.
- It is generally believed that a green products consumer faces fewer problems.
- Consumers' level of satisfaction towards green products influences their preference of continuing to buy green products in future.
- There exists a close association between consumers' attitude towards eco-friendliness and their awareness towards green products.
- There exists a close association between attitude exhibited by the consumers while purchasing of green products and their awareness towards them.
- There exists a close association between consumers' awareness towards green products and factors that motivated them to buy the green products.
- There exists a close association between factors that motivated consumers to buy the green products and the nature of product bought by them.
- There exists a close association between consumers' attitude towards eco-friendliness and the nature of products bought by them.
- There exists a close association between consumers' attitude towards green products and the nature of products bought by them.
- There exists a close association between consumers' perception towards green products and the nature of products bought by them.
- There exists a close association between consumers' satisfaction towards green products and the nature of products bought by them.

1.8. Research Methodology

The present study is both explorative and descriptive in nature and it has applied both quantitative and qualitative techniques of research for data analysis. The study has been conducted in two phases. In the first stage, large number of literature reviews were collected and assessed. This stage of the research is quite quantitative in nature. The second phase of data collection were mostly based on qualitative techniques i.e., in-depth interviews were conducted among the sample respondents with the support of a well-structured questionnaire to examine the hypotheses of the study.

1.8.1. *Study Area*

Coimbatore, also known as Kovai, is a major city in the Indian state of Tamil Nadu. Coimbatore is the second largest city in the state after Chennai and the sixteenth largest urban agglomeration in India. It is one of the fastest growing tier-II cities in India and a major hub for textiles, industries, commerce, education, information technology, healthcare and manufacturing in Tamil Nadu. It is often referred to as the "Manchester of South India" due to its cotton production and textile industries. Coimbatore is also referred to as the "Pump City" and it supplies nearly half of India's requirements of motors and pumps. The city is one of the largest exporters of jewellery, wet grinders, poultry and auto components with "Coimbatore Wet Grinder" and "Kovai Cora Cotton" recognised as Geographical Indications by the Government of India. In spite of its prominence as a busting industrial city, Coimbatore still remains one of the most pollution-free cities in India. Covering an area of 23.5 square kilometers, the city houses some of the biggest names in Indian Industry. The economic significance, population size and less pollution factor of this city motivated the researcher to select this region as the study area.

1.8.2. *Sampling Framework*

The study applied two different types of sampling techniques for the effective conduct of this study. To identify and define the geographical region the researcher adopted cluster based random sampling and for the collection of primary data from the sample respondents the researcher had adopted convenient sampling technique.

The total population of this district is 2916620. Out of 930882 population size: 477937 are male and 452945 are female residing in the city. The entire Coimbatore city is geographically divided into five regions: East, West, North, South and Center. Each region is subdivided into 20 wards constituting a total of 100 wards. A sample of twenty - five per cent i.e. 25 wards was chosen as sample. From each region (North, South, East, West and Center) of the city five wards were selected for field survey. Since the researcher encountered practical difficulties in approaching all consumers residing in the selected wards, a sample of 30 respondents from each ward has been chosen for the study which makes 150 respondents in each region that makes up a total sample size of 750 respondents from five regions of the Coimbatore city.

1.8.3. *Sample Size Justification*

From analysis of various studies conducted earlier it has been well understood that the sample size of the study is adequate. The study draws relevance of Orme. B (2010)13 sampling size definition. According to Ormer sample size for conjoint studies generally can range from about 150 to 1,200 respondents and it largely depends on the purpose of research. Conjoint analysis is a statistical technique used in Social Science (marketing, management and others) research to determine how people value different attributes (feature, function, benefits) that make up an individual product or service. Based on this concept, the sampling framework of the study is constructed.

1.8.4. Sources of Data

The data collections are divided into two stages for effective conduct of the research work. In the first stage, the researcher largely concentrated on the review of secondary data of available literature, which forms a part of the desk research work. The secondary data was also collected from the text books, research works, journals, newspapers and websites. Primary data were collected with the help of a well-structured questionnaire.

1.8.5. Data Reliability and Validity

The reliability of an indicator can be defined as its overall quality, i.e. its consistency and its ability to give the same results in repeated measurement. The most outstanding feature of reliability is the test-retest correlation of the specific measure under scrutiny.

Correspondingly, the test-retest correlation for most single-item measures is presented in the following table.

Table 1.1: Data Validity & Reliability Test

General Variables	Number of Items	Range	Cronbach's Alpha
Consumers' level of attitude towards green products	5	1-5	.813
Nature of green attitude exhibited by consumers while making purchase decision	12	1-5	.825
Buying green products	13	1-13	.712
Perception towards green products	9	1-5	.807
Satisfaction towards green products and its marketing practices	11	1-5	.773
Agreeability about benefits obtained by buying green products	10	1-5	.743
Overall score for sample adequacy (Kaiser -Meyer-Olkin measure of sampling adequacy)	.761		
Overall score for data reliability (Cronbach's Alpha)	.779		

Source: Computed from Primary Data

The validity test aims to measure the extent to which differences in scores reflect differences in the measured characteristic. Predictive validity is a measure of the usefulness of a measuring instrument as a predictor. Proof of predictive validity is determined by the correlation between results and actual behaviour. Construct validity is the extent to which a measuring instrument measures what it intends to measure. The acceptable value for KMO is greater than or equal to 0.50 (Kaiser H., 1970). This is found to be 0.761 in the present study which is inacceptable ranges (Table 1.1). The most widely used measure to assess the internal consistency of constructs is Cronbach's alpha.

The generally agreed upon value of Cronbach's alpha is 0.700, although it may decrease to 0.600 in the case of exploratory research (Hair et al. 2006; pp.137). In this research the reliability measure for the whole scale is .779 which is acceptable. Again the reliability for all the constructs is shown in Table 1.1; the values for all the constructs range between 0.813-.712, which is acceptable. Hence, the construct reliability in this research is satisfactory. The result of Cronbach's alpha draws a significant amount of correlation between the variables tested.

1.9. Operational Concept

Some of the operational concepts used in this study:

- **Green Products:** The word green means products that do not harm the earth or environment. These products, also called sustainable products, provide benefits for the people economically, socially, environmentally, while preserving the public health. These products are environmentally safe from its extraction of raw materials to production, consumption and disposal. Eco-products are also known as environment-friendly products or green products as they cause minimal harm to people and the environment.

- **Green Consumers:** A consumer who buys products that are environment-friendly is termed as a green consumer. A green consumer does not buy any product that has a direct or an indirect adverse effect on the environment.

- **Green Products:** The term green products can be used in case of recycling, renewable, toxic-free or biodegradable resources i.e., energy, materials, or ingredients. Green products can be identified by following measures: (i) Products those are originally grown. (ii) Products those are recyclable, reusable and biodegradable. (ii) Products with natural ingredients. (iv) Products containing recycled contents and non-toxic chemical (v) Products contents under approved chemicals (vi) Products that do not harm or pollute the environment (vii) Products that will not be tested on animals (viii) Products that have green packaging i.e. reusable, refillable containers ect.

- **Green Marketing:** Green marketing is also called environmental marketing/ecological marketing. "Green Marketing" also refers to holistic marketing concept wherein the production, marketing consumption and disposal of products and services happen in a manner that is less detrimental to the environment with growing awareness about the implications of global warming, non-biodegradable solid waste, harmful impact of pollutants etc.

- **Green Attributes:** The Greenness of products is defined through various attributes. These could be environmentally focussed in terms of materials used, energy consumed or pollution generated. These attributes are reflected in different stages of the life cycle –before usage, during usage or after usage 1.

- **Green Awareness:** Green Awareness has become one of the reasons for consumers to show their responsibility to protect the environment prior to purchasing activities. Consumers with green awareness in mind are also willing to pay extra because they understand the environmental benefits that can be gained from the product. In fact, green products give an impression of being compatible to the environmentally friendly lifestyle hence becoming a catalyst for a more positive predisposition in mind.

- **Green Commitment:** Green consumers possess a strong personal commitment to protect and improve the quality of environment in their daily routine activities. Knowing the negative impact of pollution on human being and other living creatures, consumers are becoming more responsible towards environmental protection.

- **Green Companies:** For years, consumers have shown their greatest concern about environmental issues. They demand companies to produce environmentally friendly products with minimum impact to the environment. Green companies with high reputation believe in sustainable marketing and consistently protect the environment for the benefits of next generation.

- **Green Experience:** Experience and knowledge about green products can be another reason for the consumers to purchase green products. Easy access to information provides more knowledge about ecological issues. In the meantime, product consumption offers greater understanding about the ingredient, usage and impact to the environment. With such involvement consumers tend to position a clearer concept of green product in their mind. This cognitive learning process enables them to evaluate the green product and making a comparison with the existing ones. As a result, the benefit of green products can be traced and the next course of action can be taken.

- **Green Circle:** Consumers' purchase decision is commonly influenced by the opinion of people around them (i.e. family members, friends and community). Social interactions and communication network have made the consumers realize the importance of green products. During the interaction process, they receive and share various types of information about products in the marketplace. They continuously evaluate the value of the product based on comments and opinions expressed by participants in the social system 1.

1.10. Statistical Tools Applied

The following tools are expected to be applied in the study: Frequency distribution, Weighted Average, Chi-Square Test, One-way ANOVA, Independent "Z" Test, Kendall's Co-efficient of Concordance, Multiple Regressions, Rotation factor analysis, Reliability Test and Structural Equation Model.

- Frequency distribution supported the researcher for calculation of percentage-wise distribution of frequency i.e., number of sample for each variable.
- Weighted arithmetic means and Likert's Summated scales helped in interpreting the averages of the variable used in this study like: consumers' level of attitude towards green products, nature of green attitude exhibited by the consumers while making purchase decision, consumers' level of perceptions and satisfaction towards green products and level of agreeability expressed by the consumers about benefits obtained by buying green products.
- Chi-Square test was performed to measure whether the consumers' level of awareness towards green products support them in recognising products as green or not.
- Kendall's Co-Efficient of Concordance was performed to justify the fact that the factors that influence consumers for buying green products differ from one individual to another.
- One-Way ANOVA test was performed to reveal a descriptive analysis on the consumer's level of awareness towards green products and their demographic and socio-economic status. The same test was applied to measure consumers' level of agreeability about benefits obtained by buying green products among their demographic and socio–economic status of the sample group.
- Independent Z-test was computed to list out the nature of problems faced by the consumers while buying green products.

- The multiple regression analysis was performed to identify whether there exists an association between: (i) Consumers' level of awareness towards green products influences their level of attitude towards it. (ii) Consumers' level of attitude towards green products and their level of perceptions towards it. (iii) Consumers' level of perception towards green products and level of satisfaction towards it. (iv) Consumers' level of satisfaction towards green products influences their preference of continuing to buy green products in future.

SEM model was performed to measure the prevailing association between:

- Consumers' attitude towards eco-friendliness and their awareness towards green products.
- Attitude exhibited by the consumers while purchase of green products and their awareness towards it.
- Consumers' awareness towards green products and factors that motivated them to buy the green products.
- Factors that motivated consumers to buy the green products and the nature of products bought by them.
- Consumers' attitude towards eco-friendliness and the nature of products bought by them. Consumers' attitude towards green products and the nature of products bought by them. Consumers' perception towards green products and the nature of products bought by them.
- Rotation Factor Analysis and Reliability Analysis tests were conducted to measure factors that (i) factors that influence the consumers to buy green products (ii) consumers' level of perception towards green products (iii) consumers' level of satisfaction towards green products and (iv) consumers' level of agreeability about benefits obtained by buying green products.

1.11. Limitations of the Study

Generally, during conduct of social research work the researchers encounter limitations like: restriction in selection of geographical regions, lack of adequate information on a given subject due to variables etc. This study suffers from the geographic limitation and sample size limitation.

- Geographical scope of the study was limited to Coimbatore city and the study does not represent the whole of Tamil Nadu or India.

- Similarly, the sample size of the study was restricted to 750 respondents, which is very small. Hence the small size and geographic limitation may influence the study in generalisation of the findings and its universal application.
- Yet another limitation of the study was that the data collected in the present study may not be free from the errors in primary data sources like: biased information provided by the respondents, lack of their knowledge about services and others. This again may influence the study findings and the conclusion drawn by the researcher, which is out of the control.

1.12. Chapter Organisation Scheme

Chapter design is an inevitable part of any thesis work. Chapter organisation framework of this research work has been structured to gain insights into the above purpose and thus includes five chapters, namely the Introduction and Research Design, Literature Review, Theoretical discussion, Analysis and Discussion, Summary, Findings, Suggestions, Conclusion, and Future Research Scope for the Study. The thesis of the study is organised into five major chapters. A brief outline of the chapters is discussed below.

Chapter I: The introductory chapter deals with the: introduction, significance of the study, statement of the problem, scope of the study, conceptual framework of the study, objectives of the study, hypotheses of the study, research methodology, statistical tools applied, limitation of the study and chapterisation scheme.

Chapter II: The second chapter reviews selected literature relating to study concept and objectives framed for the effective conduct of this study.

Chapter III: The third chapter consists of an elaborate theoretical discussion on the subject issues. This chapter is titled "Overview of Green Marketing: Consumers' Attitude and Preferences towards Green Products".

Chapter IV: The fourth chapter consists of analysis and interpretation of the surveyed data.

Chapter V: The fifth chapter contains summary of the study, findings of the research, implications and scope for future research studies.

CHAPTER II

REVIEW OF LITERATURE

2.1. Introduction

A detailed review of literature was carried out to have a clear knowledge about the research subject, to find out the research gap and to identify the relevant researchable issues for the study. The review began by identifying previous research topics on green marketing, consumers' awareness and attitude towards green marketing and green products and also on consumers' perception and buying behaviour towards green products. This study aims to identify the prevailing gaps in the studies conducted in the past and to streamline the scope and objectives for the conduct of this study.

2.2. Green Products

Between 1980 and 1990, a trend in "green products" appeared, and this type of niche products occupied a distinct place in the market. But only at the beginning of the 21st century, marked with global warming and natural resource depletion, "green" started influencing the practices of product manufacturers and the consumers too.

Mebratu (2001) claims that a green product possesses environmental procurement: systematically building environmental considerations in to day-to-day procurement decision-making and operations. Dantas et al. (2004) this research paper aimed to analyse the influences of packaging on the consumer's choice towards green products. The study found that consumers' choice for green products is heavily influenced by the product package. The study commented that packaging attributes can persuade consumers to purchase the product. The study found that though packages and labels have only a few seconds of impact on the consumer's mind i.e. during shopping, it may catch the consumer's attention and convince the shopper to buy a product that is placed on the self of a retail store.

Gurau and Ranchhod (2005) define green products as "a product that was manufactured using toxic-free ingredients and environmental-friendly procedures, and which is certified as such by a recognised organisation" Gan et al. (2008) study aimed to analyse consumers' purchasing behaviour towards green products in New Zealand. The study found that consumers who are environmentally conscious are more likely to purchase green products. The study findings also revealed the fact that traditional product attributes such as price, quality, and brand are still the most important attributes that consumers consider while purchasing green products. The study concluded by stating that green product attributes play a very important role in product development since they affect consumer product choices and they help marketers to satisfy customers' needs, wants and demands. The study also stated that all types of consumers both individual and industrial are becoming more concerned and aware of the natural environment.

According to the Organisation for Economic Co-operation and Development (OECD) (2009) green products are the ones produced without non-toxic chemicals or are recyclable, reusable, bio-degradable or having eco-friendly packaging and with low detrimental environmental impact at all stages of its lifecycle with the long-term goal of preservation of natural environment.

Nurse et al. (2010) study aimed to analyse the motivation and buying behaviour of the consumers towards green products. The study found that consumers' buying decision of green products depends on their: attitude, social perception, consumer effectiveness, availability, current purchase behaviour (willingness to pay higher price WTP), and perceived behaviour control.

Pavan (2010) defines green product, "as incorporation of the following characteristics: originally grown; recyclable, reusable and bio-degradable; with natural ingredients; possesses recycled content, non-toxic chemical; does not harm or pollute the environment; it is not tested on animals and have eco-friendly packaging i.e., reusable, refillable containers and others.

According to Peter (2011) green products were products that guaranteed that they were produced in a more environmental friendly way that minimizes the impact of the environment as opposed to their non-green or conventional equivalents.

Mohanasundaram (2012) in his article entitled "Green Marketing-Challenges and Opportunities" had commented that the products that are manufactured through green technology and that caused no environmental hazards are called green products. Promotion of green technology and green products is necessary for protection of natural resources and sustainable development of human kind.

According to Green Purchasing Network of India (2014) greenness of products is defined through various attributes. These could be environmentally focused in terms of materials used, energy consumed or pollution generated. These attributes are reflected in different stages of the life cycle before usage, during usage or after usage.

Yusuf and Fatima's (2015) research study aimed to explore the concept of green marketing, or green products in relation to consumers' behaviour. The study found that large population think that eco-friendly products are good for the environment and are also healthy for them as consumers. The study comments that eco-friendly products are of good quality and the performances of these products are better than the conventional products.

Padmaja and Mohan (2016) study claims that Green products may range from food products to clothing and electronics, to automobiles and buildings; every product can be made green by changing the raw-material and processes.

2.3. Understanding the Concept of Green Marketing and its Definitions

Green marketing refers to holistic marketing concept wherein the product, marketing consumption on disposal of products and services happen in a manner that is less detrimental to the environment with growing awareness about the implications of global warming, non-biodegradable solid waste, harmful impact of pollutants etc. At present, scenario both marketers and consumers are becoming increasingly sensitive to the need for switch into green products and services. Few reviews pertaining to this concept of green marketing is discussed in this study.

According to Peattie (2001) the evolution of green marketing has three phases. First phase was termed as "Ecological" green marketing, and during this period all marketing activities were concerned to help to resolve environmental problems and provide remedies for environmental problems. Second phase was "Environmental" green marketing and the focus shifted on clean technology that involved designing of innovative new products, which takes care of pollution and waste issues. Third phase was "Sustainable" green marketing.It came into prominence in the late 1990s and early 2000. During 1990s, the concern for environmental protection increased and as a result it increased the challenges for the companies to sell eco-friendly products in more reliable and trusted means.

According to Ginsberg and Bloom (2004) green marketing has not lived up to the hopes and dreams of many social activists. The study commented although public opinion polls consistently show that consumers would prefer to choose a green product over one that is less friendly to the environment, but, there are a few substitutes that come to the mind of consumers, when they tend to buy an eco-friendly product.

D'souza (2005) study aimed to assess the impact of green advertisements on changing consumers' attitude towards green products. The study claimed that terms such as "environmentally friendly, recyclable, bio-degradable, and ozone safe" are often used regularly in green advertisements and consumers are seldom exposed to such messages effectively.

Ottman (2006) study aimed to evaluate green marketing myopia. The study identified major challenges faced by the green marketers. It also covers the internal and external opportunities which could be helpful to speed up the expansion of green marketing. Soonthonsmai (2007) study defined green marketing as the activities taken by firms that are concerned about the environment or green problems by delivering the environmentally friendly goods or services to create consumers' and society's satisfaction. The author also coins the term green marketing as social marketing, ecological marketing or environmental marketing.

Saxena and Khandelwal (2008) say green Marketing can be viewed both as a type of marketing and a marketing philosophy. As a type of marketing it is like industrial or service marketing and is concerned with marketing of a specialised kind of product, i.e. green product (including green goods such as fuel efficient cars or recycled products as well as green ideas such as "save oil" or "conserve natural habitat"). As a philosophy, green marketing runs parallel to the societal marketing concept and espouses the view that satisfied the customers. The study comments that the marketers should take into account the concept of green marketing in ecological interests of the society as a whole, but it should be part of their Corporate Social Responsibility (CSR). The study mentioned that green marketing is an attempt to characterize a product as being environmentally friendly (ecofriendly). It holds the view that marketing which is a part of business not only has to satisfy customers in particular, but also has to take into account the interests of society in general. That is, all those who are affected by the activities of a business should be kept in mind when setting the objectives and the policies of an organisation. This has already helped to increase the recent trend towards the "greening" of the companies. It is only since 1990s that the researchers have started academically analysing consumers and industries attitude towards green marketing.

Dutta's. (2009) research article aimed to identify the means through which green marketing practices can be sustained in a new imperative way. The study mentioned that green marketing involves developing good quality products which can meet consumers' needs and wants by focusing on the quality, performance, pricing and convenience all in environment-friendly ways.

Shrikanth and Raju (2012) research paper aimed to find out what actually Green Marketing is all about and how can a business firm be more competitive by using green marketing strategies to gain a competitive edge over others. The study commented that green marketing assumes even more importance and relevance in developing countries in the world like India which should be path-breakers and trendsetters for all to follow. The study suggested that consumers, industrial buyers and suppliers need to take positive effects to promote green marketing in order to protect the environments.

Manjunath and Manjunath (2013) research paper aimed to study the theoretical concepts of the green marketing, green marketing management and green products. The paper also studied the theory contributed by various researchers in the area of environment marketing that includes green products, green customers, green marketing mix and ecological processes. The research paper concluded by stating that business firms need to change their mindset from traditional marketing strategies to green marketing strategies in order to survive in the green competitive world and to have a positive impact on the environment through green marketing elements.

Azam's (2014) research paper draws a detailed discussion on the key issues of green marketing. The study stated that now corporates as well as consumers have become more concerned with the issues of green marketing practices at various levels of their business. Green marketing emerged as an umbrella term in modern marketing which incorporates all the activities related to marketing, like production, packaging, etc.

Nath et al. (2014) study aimed to examine the relationship of green marketing promotion tools such as environmental advertising and eco-labeling on Indian consumers' intention to purchase a green product. The study found that green advertising and eco-labelling has significant positive relations to green purchase intentions. Whereas, consumers skepticism behaviour towards green marketing promotion tools has no significant effect on green purchase intentions.

Kumar and Yamuna's (2014) research paper aimed to introduce terms and concepts of environment marketing and ecological marketing. The study aims to provide information on why the green marketing emerged, and through which media it has been emerged. The study stated that a consumer's demographic and socio-economic character positively influences their purchase of green products. The study suggested the marketers to attract more consumers by making appealing call that: green products are low-priced and eco-friendly, green products generally use eco-friendly materials and it is energy-efficient, thereby causing less or no detrimental impact on the environment. The study also comments that the eco-friendly products contain no harmful elements and suggested to the public to use green products as they are usually biodegradable and made from recyclable materials.

Singh and Singh (2015) this paper provides an overview of green marketing, need and significance of green practices. The authors comment that the term green marketing is the hottest cake in today's scenario for all business activities. Environmental degradation all over the world is a significant problem. The study commented that natural resources are exploited at fullest without any consideration of their repercussions.

These natural resources are limited and human wants are unlimited. Thus, to protect the environment and natural resources, governments, NGOs (Non-Governmental Organisation) and international organisations have created pressure on marketers to fulfil their responsibilities towards these ecological issues. Due to long efforts and pressures made by these stakeholders, many companies are practising green marketing.

2.4. Role of Marketers in Selling Green Products

Companies that develop new and improved products and services with environment inputs in mind give themselves access to new markets, increase their profit sustainability, and enjoy a competitive advantage over the companies which are not concerned for the environment. Those companies, who are actively using green marketing must ensure that their activities are not misleading to consumers or industries, and do not breach any of the regulations or laws dealing with environmental marketing. In this section of the study reviews on the role of marketers in selling green products have been discussed.

Karna et al. (2003) study aimed to assess the social responsibility of marketers in environmental marketing planning. The study found that proactive marketers are the most genuine group in implementing environmental marketing voluntarily and seeking competitive advantage through environmental friendliness. The study results also provided evidence that green values, environmental marketing strategies, structures and functions are logically connected to each other.

Mishra and Sharma's (2010) study found that consumers of green products are willing to pay more prices to maintain a cleaner and greener environment. The study comments that marketers have the responsibility to make the consumers understand the need for and benefits of green products as compared to non-green ones. This research paper discussed how businesses have increased their rate of targeting green consumers, those who are concerned about the environment and allow it to affect their purchasing decisions. The study identified the three particular segments of green consumers and explores the challenges and opportunities businesses have with green marketing.

Unruh.G and Ettenson R (2010) research article discussed three smart paths to developing sustainable green products. The authors have introduced and described three broad strategies that companies can use to align their green goals with their capabilities: Accentuate: Strategy involves playing up existing or latent green attributes in the company's current portfolio. Acquire: Strategy involves buying someone else, green brand and marketing it. Architect: Strategy involves architecting green offerings i.e. building green products from scratch.

According to Ramanakumar et al. (2012) the current rapid growth in the economy and the patterns of consumer's consumption and behaviour worldwide are the main causes of environmental deterioration. The shortage of natural resource, which seriously affects human beings existence and development, environment protection has become the worldwide focus. The growing social and regulatory concerns for the environment lead an increasing number of customers to consider green issues as a major source of strategic change. Rising awareness of global environment and social problems has forced companies to recognize these demands in their activities. Now, industries are increasingly being required to meet social and environmental specifications in the market because of rising customer pressures. Even though it increased eco-awareness of customers during past few decades, there are some barriers to the diffusions of more ecologically oriented consumption and production styles. Therefore companies are increasingly recognising the importance of green marketing concepts. Green marketing is the need of the hour as world is experiencing environmental degradation every single day. A few reviews on the manufacturers and retailers focus towards green products and green marketing is discussed in the section of the study.

Kumar (2013) study had stated that majority of Indian companies and government agencies are not concerned about the green marketing and environmental protection. Therefore green marketing is still in its infancy stage and a lot of research has to be conducted on green marketing to fully explore its potential. Marketers also have the responsibility to make the consumers understand the need and benefits of green products in comparison to non-green ones.

Rajeev Kumar (2015) aimed to understand the concept of green marketing for the companies and its long-term impact on the business profitability. The study found that the companies that have favourable attitude towards green product and green marketing help in improving the sales and the image of the companies. In addition to the positive image of the company green marketing also harmonizes environmental and individual interests of the company. Those companies who want to keep up with the development of green marketing and fulfilling their social expectations, need to get to know green marketing and its opportunities in the 21st century deeper. It is also believed by many companies that if they will offer green products to the consumers it will give them a competitive advantage over their competitors, as people these days have a positive attitude towards green products.

2.5. Consumers' Awareness and Attitude towards Green Marketing and Products

Growing awareness among consumers world over about environmental issues has significantly influenced their attitude to environment and its protection. Environmental attitude is identified as the judgment an individual has towards the protection and promotion of the environment. Green marketing depends on the consumer's awareness and attitude towards the environment. Few reviews of yesteryear studies on the consumers' awareness and attitude towards green products and marketing is discussed in this section of the study.

Laroche et al. (2002) study aimed to discuss the cultural differences in environmental knowledge, attitudes and behaviours of Canadian consumers. The study finding revealed that ecologically conscious consumers believe that current environmental conditions are deteriorating and represent serious problems related to the security of the world. On the contrary, consumers who are less sensible to ecological issues perceive that environmental problems will solve themselves. The study concludes by stating that consumers' attitude towards environmental issues does influence their environmentally friendly purchasing behaviour.

Leire and Thidell (2005) study aimed to analyse the consumer's awareness towards purchase of green products. The study found that consumers' awareness of eco-labelling does not influence their green purchase decisions. D'Souza et al. (2006) study aimed to investigate the green products and corporate strategy of companies. The study found that some consumers considered the information given on product labels inaccurate and therefore they do not rely on the labels while making purchasing decisions of green products. The study also observed that lower quality and inconvenience to use green products significantly influence consumers' buying behaviour.

Soonthorsmai (2007) study aimed to assess the issue of environmental and green marketing in relevance with global competitive marketing practices. The study found that consumers are increasingly aware and concerned about the essentials of environmental issues and they tend to buy more green products.

Rahim's (2009) research study aimed to assess the consumers' intention and factors affecting green food consumption in Malaysia. The study findings indicated that the consumers express positive attitude toward green food and they are more concerned about the environmental issues and health consciousness.

Verma and Verma's (2011) paper attempted to assess the awareness level of green marketing among Indian consumers. The study findings revealed that awareness level about green marketing was quite high among the consumers surveyed. The study found that consumers are more aware of branded products compared to unbranded products. The study also found that customer satisfaction towards green products got a poor rating as more than 75 per cent of the customers believed that companies need to do more to satisfy them. The study suggests that the manufacturers need to improve the quality of the product and their after -sales service.

Cherian and Jolly Jacob (2012) study introduced the concept of green marketing and threw light into the various ways in which the different consumer attributes are related to the concept of green marketing. Based on the extensive literature reviews the study commented that majority of the consumers still lack 'green' knowledge and because of such low awareness towards green products organisations are still not pushing towards developing more green products nor are they working hard on green packaging. The study stated that organisations still believe that marketing aspects such as developing a proper supply chain, packaging, pricing etc take precedence over green marketing initiatives.

Veluri's (2012) research paper aimed to investigate consumers' beliefs and attitudes towards environment protection and their purchasing behaviour of eco-friendly products. The study identified that consumers are not exposed enough to green product marketing communication. The study suggested that the Indian market of greener products can increase their market share among the consumer groups through strengthening their pro-environmental values, brands building and effective marketing strategies.

Ling's (2013) research paper aimed to examine factors that influence consumers' purchase intention towards green personal care products. The study finding revealed that environmental attitudes and self-efficacy were found to be the factors that drive the green product purchase intention of consumers. In addition, the study found that consumers' willingness to pay more for green personal care products moderately influences their environmental attitudes and purchase intention.

Suki's (2013) research study aimed to examine the influence of consumers' environmental concerns, awareness about green product, price and influences of brand image on their purchasing decision of green products. The study findings revealed that consumers' awareness of price and brand image significantly influences their purchasing decision of green products.

Maheshwari's (2014) research paper focused to assess the success of efforts put by marketers in bringing green brands awareness in consumer's mind. The study further reviewed consumer behaviour and impact of marketing communication to identify how consumers are persuaded to opt for greener products. The study identified that consumers are not exposed enough to green product marketing communication and suggests the greater use of marketing and brands to promote and sell products that are environmentally friendly and function effectively. The paper suggested that the Indian market for greener products could be exploited more within consumer groups that have pro- environmental values.

Yusuf and Fatima (2015) study aimed to analyse the consumers' attitude and perception towards green products. The study observed that large population thinks that eco-friendly products are good for the environment and are also healthy for them. Eco-friendly products are good in quality and the performances of these products are better than the conventional products.

Sharma and Trivedi's (2016) researcher paper attempted to identify variables and the effect of each variable on consumer's green buying behaviour. The study identified eight variables, namely eco-labels, eco-brands, environmental advertising, environmental awareness, green product, green price and green promotions and demographic features of consumers that directly affect green consumers' buying behaviour. The study found that each variable is equally significant for the green marketer. The study findings also reveal that there are enough evidences available and it clearly states that all the green marketing variables affect consumers in a positive way towards the purchase of green products; the marketers should take a keen note of them in order to get the best marketing strategy. The study suggested that the marketers should know which variable treats more impact on the consumers buying behaviour.

2.6. Consumers' Perception and Buying Behaviour towards Green Marketing

From the discussion in the previous section it has been understood that green marketing emerges from societal marketing (Kotler,1999). "Green Marketing" refers to holistic marketing concept wherein the production, marketing, consumption and disposal of products and services happen in a manner that is less detrimental to the environment with growing awareness about the implications of global warming, non-biodegradable solid waste, harmful impact of pollutants, etc. Both marketers and consumers are becoming increasingly sensitive to the need for a switch into green products and services. In this section studies related to consumer perception and buying behaviour towards green marketing have been reviewed.

Kollmuss and Agyeman (2002) study aimed to evaluate the environment-friendly behaviour among the consumers. The study reported that the eco-sensitive consumer consciously seeks to minimize the negative impact of one's actions on the natural resources, to minimise resource and energy consumption, to use non-toxic substances and aims to reduce waste production. The study described that environmental consciousness is influenced by two sets of determinants: external determinants like: media, family and culture and the internal determinants include: demographics and psychology of a consumer. The study found that consumers' ecological buying behaviour is influenced by four factors: environmental consciousness, willingness to pay higher price for eco-products, perceived environmental characteristics of a product and company's environmental reputation.

Mostafa (2007) research study aimed to analyse the influence of gender differences among the consumers of green products in Egypt. The findings of the study states that green purchasing behaviour refers to the consumption of products that are: benevolent or beneficial to the environment, recyclable or conservable; or sensitive or responsive to ecological concerns. The study found that gender does not influence the consumers' buying behaviour towards green products.

Mehta et al. (2011) in their research study attempted to study the impact of gender of adolescent consumers' buying behaviour of green products in Indore city. The study findings revealed that the common approaches towards green products are very rational and they are not sufficiently motivated to make an environmentally friendly purchase decision. The study observed that adolescent consumers of Indore city are against harmful chemicals usage in their day-to-day life and they encourage usage and production of green products. The study suggests that it is high time to bring out the consciousness of the public about using only eco-friendly products. The study concludes by stating that green i.e., eco-friendly products will offer a better tomorrow and a safe working environment for the next generation. The present study suggests to the marketers that the key to successful green marketing among adolescents lies in the effective use of emotional appeals in the marketing messages, peer networking to create mass/mouth-to-mouth publicity and gender-based market segmentation.

Vernekar and Wadhwa's (2011) exploratory study examined differences among ecologically-concerned and non-ecologically-concerned consumers with respect to their personal and social characteristics, and their perceptions towards marketing of green products. The study also aimed to investigate the consumers' attitudes and perceptions towards eco-friendly products in FMCG sector and their willingness to pay more for green products. The study found that there exist significant differences between consumers' attitudes and personality traits among green and non-green consumers. The study findings also revealed that the green products have substantial awareness among urban Indian customers and they are willing to pay more price for green products. The study stated that majority of customers considered that package is the most important element for green products.

Mahesh (2013) study aimed to analyse the consumers' perceived value, attitude and purchase intention of green products. The study findings reveal that the most of the consumers perceive that the green products have consistent quality, acceptable standard of quality and value for money. The consumers who have higher education levels and higher monthly income have higher perceived value towards green products. Besides the middle-aged consumers and employees of private sector have more perceived value towards green products. The studies observed that majority of the consumers are more concerned with the food safety, the protection of the environment and animal welfare. The consumers who have higher education levels and higher monthly income are more likely to purchase green products. The study found that the middle-aged consumers and employees of private sector have more intention in purchasing of green products. The perceived value, attitude purchase intention towards green products is also moderately and positively associated with each other. The study indicated that reasonable price, value for money and acceptable quality of standards are positively influencing the consumer's purchase intention of green products at one per cent level of significance. Moreover, environmental friendliness and food safety are also found to be positively influencing the consumers' purchase intention of green products at five per cent level of significance.

Agyeman's (2014) empirical study aimed to investigate the relationship between variables that affect consumers' buying behaviour of green products. The study aimed to identify the influences of price on consumers desire to pay for green products. The study also attempts to examine the factors that affect the green products' buying behaviours of the consumers. The findings of the study reveal that there exist significant relationships between the variables which affect consumers' buying behaviour towards green products. The study found that the factors affecting the consumers' buying behaviour have major implications on purchasing decisions. The study suggested to the green marketers to identify and design marketing mix strategies that may be appealing to the market segments of green products.

Nagaraju and Thejaswini (2014) research study aimed to evaluate the market awareness of eco-friendly products in Mysore district. The study also aimed to analyse the consumers' perception towards eco-friendly products and to assess consumers' willingness to pay more for eco-friendly products. The study found that nearly 93.30 per cent of the respondents are aware of the eco-friendly FMCG (Fast-Moving Consumer Goods) products. Similarly, 68.30 per cent of the respondents consider that their purchase is rational from the environmental point of view. Nearly 65 per cent of the respondents consider that their product and its packages are designed to be recycled. While making a purchase decision most of the consumers considers eco-label as a major tool in identifying eco-friendly FMCG products. The study findings also revealed that 71.70 per cent of the respondents' purchase decision changes when they see the eco-friendly labels. It has been found that consumers seek more information while buying the eco-friendly FMCG products. Most of the respondents are found to be satisfied with the quality/performance of the eco-friendly FMCG products compared with conventional products. Majority of the consumers feel that price of the eco-friendly FMCG products is higher when it is compared with non-eco-friendly FMCG products and only 63.30 per cent of them are willing to pay more for the products. The study suggests that the government organisations and the customers have to join hands together in creating awareness about eco-friendly products among the common man.

Singh et al. (2014) study aimed to find out the behaviour of consumers' toward green product and its related information. The study findings indicate that consumers who are already buying eco-friendly products and those who are satisfied by the previous purchases are willing to repeat the purchases. The study established relation with consumer satisfaction and purchase intention. Furthermore, WOM (Word-of-Mouth) and Advertisement about green products influence consumers' belief on green claim and their purchase intentions. The study found that consumers' positive attitudes concerning willingness to pay an extra price for green products are also correlated with purchase intention. However, the study indicated that positive attitudes towards green products do not always lead to action i.e. purchase of these products. The study findings demonstrated that there were differences in attitudes and purchase intentions toward green products between mainly the women and men.

Sharaf et al. (2015) research study aimed to examine the influence of price, time, and eco-label on the intention of future green products purchasing among youth in Malaysia. The study results revealed that price and time factors have a significant relationship with young consumers' intention to purchase green products. The study also observed that eco-label does not influence consumers' intention to purchase green products.

Ranganathan and Ramya (2016) study aimed to analyse the consumers' perception towards green products in Coimbatore city. The study findings confirmed that a person who has some concern for the environment would have a stronger preference for purchasing green products. The study suggested to the marketers to aggressively develop green product messages that would stimulate interest among the young generation. It is suggested to the consumers to easily differentiate green products from the non-green products based on the labels. Further, it was suggested to markets that the price the green products should be changed as affordable to encourage purchase.

2.7. Challenges and Opportunities of Green Products Marketing

With the threat of global warming looming large, it is extremely important that green marketing becomes the norm rather than an exception or just a fad. Marketers also have the responsibility to make the consumers understand the need for and benefits of green products as compared to non-green ones. Finally, consumers, industrial buyers and suppliers need to pressurize effects on minimizing the negative effects on the environment-friendly products. From this discussion it has been understood that the challenges in green marketing are more. A few reviews pertaining to this concept is discussed in this section of the study.

Sudhir Sachdev's (2011) research study aimed to explore why people do not buy environmentally friendly products and the study also aimed to find out the main constraints that restrict them from buying green products. The study found that more than 50 per cent of consumers remain suspicious of green products available in the market i.e. they suspect the environmental claims i.e., false claim about the product, unsubstantiated and/or unethical marketing practices. Moreover, the study found that many consumers remain confused about which products are better for society and the environment. The study also states that in regard to eco-labelling, many experts have claimed that consumers are confused due to inappropriate labelling. The study has found that consumers do not always understand environmentally friendly labels attached to products. Eco-labels such as biodegradable, sustainable, fair wage/fair trade, environmentally friendly and recyclable are usually unfamiliar and/or unknown to consumers.

Satpal Singh's (2012) research paper aimed to examine the notion of 'green marketing' and the challenges which are associated with different aspects of green marketing in the present scenario. The study commented that Green Marketing is posing some challenges which require innovative technology so that the 'green products' can fetch wider market at domestic and international levels. It requires a periodic review of the 'green product', so that the products may become 'ecologically viable' as well as 'economically viable' for the consumers, especially those who belong to middle and low income groups.

Singal et al. (2013) research paper aimed to explore the challenges and opportunities businesses have with green marketing. The research paper also describes the reason why companies are adopting it and concludes that green marketing is something that will continuously grow in both practice and demand. The study that found that only 5 per cent of the marketing messages from "Green" campaigns is entirely true and there is a lack of standardization to authenticate these claims. They established that there exists no standardisation currently in place to certify a product as organic. Unless some regulatory bodies are involved in providing the certifications there will not be any verifiable means. A standard quality control board needs to be in place for such labelling and licensing.

Gupta et al.'s (2014) research paper highlighted the current scenario of Indian market and explores the challenges and opportunities of businesses in regard to green marketing. The study observed that consumers strongly expressed that they are familiar with green brand and have shown a keen interest to know more about green branding. The study mentioned that at present Indians are experiencing a transition from regular marketing to green brands and it is a very difficult phase. Though it is an undeniable fact that most of the consumers have realised the importance of green branding, they are highly price-sensitive. But there is a positive sign for betterment of business for green products in the near future.

Kumar et al. (2016) research paper attempted to introduce the concept of green-marketing by examining the primary reasons that make the organisations interested to adopt green marketing philosophy and the study also explores challenges that the organisations may face to implement green marketing. The study commented that with the threat of global warming looming large, it is extremely important that green marketing becomes the norm rather than an exception. The study commented that recycling of paper, metals, plastics, etc., in a safe and environmentally harmless circumstance have become much more systematized and universal. It has become the general norm to use energy-efficient lamps and other electrical goods. The study commented that environmental problems in India are growing rapidly. For the success of "Green Mantra" and creating the awareness regarding it, publicity is very essential. The programme regarding awareness about green marketing is expected by the people too. For this purpose, with the help of Ministry of Environment at Central as well as State level, many promotional activities should be carried out like: a rally at school- primary, secondary and college level, road shows, involvement of media, active participation of NGOs and many others. The study concluded by stating that it is the right time to implement the green marketing for long -term growth of the economy.

Mangai P and Subramaniam K (2017) study aimed to assess the efficacy of green marketing on refinement of Indian companies. The study commented about the importance of green marketing in India. The study stated that although many companies in India have adopted this there are too many challenges because of which this concept is still blurred, so this review also describes the challenges and opportunities of adopting Green marketing concept.

2.8. Conclusion–Research Gap

The study has provided an elaborate literature reviews on the following topics: green products, green marketing conceptual understanding and definitions, role of marketers in selling green products, consumers' awareness and attitude towards green marketing and products, consumers' perception and buying behaviour towards green marketing and challenges and opportunities of green products marketing. From the elaborate literature review it has been inferred that though many studies have been conducted in the past on the green products and green marketing, still these concepts are in the nascent stage as far as India is considered. The past studies have also confirmed that fact that the person who has some concern for the environment would have a stronger preference purchasing green products and others remain as silent spectators.

The past studies have also claimed that price and time factors have a significant relationship with consumers' intention to purchase green products. Moreover, there were differences in consumers' awareness level, attitudes and purchase intention of green products among different demographic sets of peoples. Based on the identified issues and dearth in the studies related to consumers' awareness, attitude and buying behaviour towards green products in Indian context, this study is deemed as rational and viable too. This study aims to analyse the consumers' attitude, preferences and buying practices towards green products. This study is focused on the green consumers living in Coimbatore City of Tamil Nadu.

CHAPTER III

OVERVIEW ON GREEN MARKETING: CONSUMERS

ATTITUDE AND PREFERENCES TOWARDS GREEN PRODUCTS

Green marketing is a phenomenon which has developed particular importance in the modern market. It has emerged as an important concept in India as in other parts of the developing and developed countries. This chapter provides a brief theoretical discussion on the concept of green marketing, its evolution and consumers' attitude and influences towards green products.

3.1. Evolution of Green Marketing Concept

The origins of the environmental movement can be traced back to different parts of the world throughout history. The environmentalist movement, in Europe, grew out of the reaction to the industrialisation, growth of cities and poor air and water quality due to industries pollution. Green marketing was given dominance after the proceedings of the first workshop on Ecological marketing held in Austin, Texas (US), in 1975. The workshop released the first book on green marketing entitled "Ecological Marketing". Several books on green marketing began to be published thereafter. The term "Green marketing" was first discussed in a seminar on "Ecological Marketing" organised by American Marketing Association (AMA) in 1975 and took its place in the literature. The term 'green marketing' came into prominence in the late 1980s and early 1990s. The first wave of green marketing occurred in the 1980s. The tangible milestone for the first wave of green marketing came in the form of published books, which were called Green Marketing. These books were authored by were by Ken Pattie (1992) in the United Kingdom and Jacquelyn Ottman (1993) in the United States of America.

Green marketing which is also alternatively known as environmental marketing and sustainable marketing, refers to an organisation's efforts at designing, promoting, pricing and distributing products that will not harm the environment. The green marketing has evolved over a period of time.

According to Peattie (2001), the evolution of green marketing has three phases.

- The First phase was termed as "Ecological" green marketing. During this period all marketing activities were concerned to help environment problems such as air pollution, oil spills, and synthetic DDT (dichloro-dipheny-trichloroethane) and provide remedies for environmental problems. This phase was focused on those industries and products that have a direct impact on the environment such as oil, mining and chemical industries.

- The Second phase focused on "Environmental" green marketing and the focus shifted on clean technology that involved designing of innovative new products, which took care of pollution and waste issues. This phase focused on products which are generally used in homes such as cleaning goods, white goods, carpets, papers etc. along with services such as banking and tourisms.

- The Third phase aimed at "Sustainable" green marketing. It came into prominence in the late 1990s and early 2000. The marketing discipline is beginning to address green marketing, not just in terms of reducing environment damage, but in pursuit to its sustainability. Companies like IBM and Mcdonalds have used their bulk purchasing power to enforce their back suppliers to improve their eco-performance at their own level and back it up with green audits 1.

3.2. United Nations Environment Programme on Environment Protection

The first United Nations Conference on the Human Environment (UNCHE) was held in Stockholm, Sweden from 5th June to 16th June, 1972. Representatives from 113 countries were present, as well as representatives from many international non-governmental organisations, intergovernmental organisations, and many other specialised agencies. This was the first United Nations conference held on the environment as well as the first major international gathering focused on human activities in relationship to the environment and this conference laid the foundation for environmental action at an international level. The conference acknowledged that the goal of reducing human impact on the environment would require extensive international co-operation, as many of the problems affecting the environment are global in nature. Following this conference, the United Nations Environmental Programme (UNEP) was launched in order to encourage United Nations agencies to integrate environmental measures into their programmes.

The United Nations Conference on the Human Environment (UNCHE) emphasised that defending and improving the environment must become a goal to be pursued by all countries. The Stockholm Declaration and Action Plan defined principles for the preservation and enhancement of the natural environment and highlighted the need to support people in this process. The Conference indicated that "industrialised" environmental problems such as: habitat degradation, toxicity and acid rain, were not necessarily relevant issues for all countries. In particular, development strategies were not meeting the needs of the poorest countries and communities.

Some of the specific issues addressed through this conference were the role which industrialized countries should have in the process of protecting the environment, stating that industrial countries should help to close the gap between them and underdeveloped countries while keeping their own priorities and the protection and improvement of the environment in mind. The conference developed a long set of recommendations to act as goals to pursue its mission. Recommendations included that governments communicate about environmental issues that have international implications (such as air pollution), that governments give attention to the training of those who plan, develop and manage settlement areas and that agencies work together to address many issues, such as access to clean water and population growth. However, it was the pending environmental problems that dominated the meeting and led to wider public environmental awareness.

3.2.1. *United Nations Environment Programme*

One of the greatest achievements of the United Nations Conference on the Human Environment (UNCHE) was the creation of the United Nations Environment Programme (UNEP), based in Nairobi, Kenya.

The mission of UNEP is "to provide leadership and encourage partnership in caring for the environment by inspiring, informing, and enabling nations and peoples to improve their quality of life without compromising that of future generations." UNEP is the voice for the environment within the United Nations system and works toward this mission by:

- Encouraging international participation and cooperation in addressing environmental issues and environmental policy
- Monitoring the status of the global environment and interpreting environmental data collected
- Creating environmental awareness in governments, society, and the private sector
- Coordinating UN activities pertaining to the environment
- Developing regional programmes for sustainability
- Helping environmental authorities, especially those in developing countries, form and implement policy
- Helping to develop international environmental law

3.2.2. *The United Nations Framework Convention on Climate Change*

The United Nations Framework Convention on Climate Change (UNFCCC or FCCC) was an international environmental treaty produced at the United Nations Conference on Environment and Development (UNCED), informally known as the Earth Summit, held in Rio de Janeiro from 3rd to 14th June 1992.

The objective of the treaty was to stabilise greenhouse gas concentrations in the atmosphere at a level that would prevent dangerous anthropogenic interference with the climate system. The treaty itself sets no mandatory limits on greenhouse gas emissions for individual countries and contains no enforcement mechanisms. In that sense, the treaty is considered legally non-binding. Instead, the treaty provides for updates (called "protocols") that would set mandatory emission limits. The principal update was the Kyoto Protocol, which has become much better known than the UNFCCC itself.

The UNFCCC was opened for signature on May 9, 1992, after an Intergovernmental Negotiating Committee produced the text of the Framework Convention as a report following its meeting in New York from 30 April to 9 May 1992. It entered into force on March 21, 1994. As of December 2009, UNFCCC had 192 parties. One of its first tasks was to establish national greenhouse gas inventories of Greenhouse Gas (GHG) emissions and removals, which were used to create the 1990 benchmark levels for accession of Annex I countries to the Kyoto Protocol and for the commitment of those countries to GHG reductions. Updated inventories must be regularly submitted by Annex I countries.

The UNFCCC is also the name of the United Nations Secretariat charged with supporting the operation of the Convention, with offices in Haus Carstanjen, Bonn, Germany. From 2006 to 2010 the head of the secretariat was Yvo de Boer; on 17th May, 2010 his successor, Christiana Figures from Costa Rica has been named. The Secretariat, augmented through the parallel efforts of the Intergovernmental Panel on Climate Change (IPCC), aims to gain consensus through meetings and the discussion of various strategies. The parties to the convention have met annually from 1995 in Conferences of the Parties (COP) to assess progress in dealing with climate change. In 1997, the Kyoto Protocol was concluded and established legally binding obligations for developed countries to reduce their greenhouse gas emissions.

Table 3.1: Annexure I, Annexure II Countries and Developing Countries

(Parties of UNFCCC Classifcation)

Annexure I Countries	**Annexure II Countries**
Industrialized countries and economies in transition	Developed countries which pay for costs of developing countries
Annexure I countries which have ratified the Protocol have committed to reduce their emission levels of greenhouse gases to targets that are mainly set below their 1990 levels. They may do this by allocating reduced annual allowances to the major operators within their borders. These operators can only exceed their allocations if they buy emission allowances, or offset their excesses through a mechanism that is agreed by all the parties to UNFCCC.	Annexure II countries are a sub-group of the Annexure I countries. They comprise the OECD members, excluding those that were economies in transition in 1992. Developing countries are not required to reduce emission levels unless developed countries supply enough funding and technology. Setting no immediate restrictions under UNFCCC serves three purposes:
	<ul><li>It avoids restrictions on their development, because emissions are strongly linked to industrial capacity</li><li>They can sell emissions credits to nations whose operators have difficulty meeting their emissions targets</li><li>They get money and technologies for low-carbon investments from Annexure II countries.</li><li>Developing countries may volunteer to become Annexure I countries when they are sufficiently developed.</li></ul>
There are 40 Annexure I countries and the European Union is also a member. These countries are classified as industrialized countries and countries in transition: Australia, Austria, Belarus, Belgium, Bulgaria, Canada, Croatia, Czech Republic, Denmark, Estonia, Finland, France, Germany, Greece, Hungary, Iceland, Ireland, Italy, Japan, Latvia, Liechtenstein, Lithuania, Luxembourg, Monaco, Netherlands, New Zealand, Norway, Poland, Portugal, Romania, Russian Federation, Slovakia, Slovenia, Spain, Sweden, Switzerland, Turkey, Ukraine, United Kingdom, United States of America.	There are 23 Annexure II countries and the European Union. Turkey was removed from the Annexure II list in 2001 at its request to recognize its economy as a transition economy. These countries are classified as developed countries which pay for costs of developing countries: Australia, Austria, Belgium, Canada, Denmark, Finland, France, Germany, Greece, Iceland, Ireland, Italy, Japan, Luxembourg, Netherlands, New Zealand, Norway, Portugal, Spain, Sweden, Switzerland, United Kingdom, United States of America

Source: Artee Aggrawal (2010), Factors Affecting Green Marketing In India: A Study of Metro Consumers, Factors Affecting Green Marketing In India-A Study of Metro Consumers Artee Agarwal.pdf.

Some opponents of the Convention argue that the split between Annexure I and developing countries is unfair, and that both developing countries and developed countries need to reduce their emissions unilaterally. Some countries claim that their costs of following the Convention requirements will stress their economy. This was one reason given by George W. Bush, the President of the United States, for not forwarding the Kyoto Protocol to the United States Senate for ratification. Other countries point to research, such as the Stern Report, that calculates the cost of compliance to be less than the cost of the consequences of doing nothing.

Since the UNFCCC entered into force, the parties have been meeting annually in Conferences of the Parties (COP) to assess progress in dealing with climate change, and beginning in the mid-1990s, to negotiate the Kyoto Protocol to establish legally binding obligations for developed countries to reduce their greenhouse gas emissions. From 2005 the Conferences have met in conjunction with Meetings of Parties of the Kyoto Protocol (MOP), and parties to the Convention that are not parties to the Protocol can participate in Protocol-related meetings as observers.

3.3. Need of Green Marketing

The biggest challenge today's manufacturers and marketers of products facing is to keep the customers as well as consumers in fold and to keep the mother natural environment safe. As there is fear that if companies do not turn eco-friendly and effectively manage the environmental issues they may lose many loyal and profitable customers. In today's innovative business environment well supported by modern high technology technologies green marketing and social responsibility has become norm of many business enterprises. Also due to growing green community and consumer interests in green products and socially responsible products, increased community pressure on companies to internalise externalities such as: health issues, neighbourhood amenity, climate change; environmental and governmental legalisations and initiatives; innovative technologies and approaches of dealing with pollution, improved resource and energy efficiency, and to retain old (loyal and profitable) customers and consumers, it is very much urgent to implement green marketing. Further green management produces new environment-friendly customers which leads to increase in sales and profits of an organisation that leads to growth and development of business. It also leads to good public image of the organisation among the common public. In the present times when the government regulations around the globe are very strict and the whole world is talking about global warming, climate change and environment protection many companies are left with no option but to adopt green marketing otherwise it might be too late to survive in the greener world. The consumer's world over in general and India in particular are increasingly buying energy efficient products. In short, most of the companies are venturing into green marketing due to the following reasons:

- In India, around 25 per cent of the consumers prefer environmental-friendly products and around 28 per cent of them are health-conscious. Therefore, green marketers have opportunity to diverse and fairly sizeable segments to cater.

- Many companies have started realising the fact that they must behave in an environment-friendly manner and should focus both in achieving environmental objectives as well as profit-related objectives.

- Various regulations recently framed by the Government of India to protect consumers and the society at large led to the adoption of Green marketing as a compulsion rather than a choice. For example, the ban of plastic bags in many parts of the country and prohibition of smoking in public areas, etc.

- In India many corporates take up green marketing to maintain their competitive edge.

3.4. Green Marketing Concept

According to American Marketing Association, "Green Marketing is the marketing of products that are presumed to be environmentally safe, involve developing and promoting products and services that satisfy customers' want and need for Quality, Performance, Affordable Pricing and Convenience without having a detrimental input on the environment". Green Marketing is also tied closely with issues of industrial ecology and environmental sustainability i.e. life cycle analysis, material use, extended producers liability, resource flows and eco-efficiency.

The green marketing is holistic marketing concepts that is incorporated with a broad range of activities i.e., production, marketing, consumption and disposal of products and services that happen in a manner that is less detrimental to the environment. The environmental list movement, at least in Europe, grew out of the reaction to industrialisation, growth of cities and poor air and water quality. According to Pride and Ferrel (1993), green marketing which is also known as environmental marketing or sustainable marketing refers to the organisation's efforts at designing, promoting, pricing and distributing products that will not harm the environment. Polonsky (1994) defines green marketing as all activities designed to generate and facilitate any exchanges intended to satisfy human needs or wants that have minimal detrimental impact on the natural environment.

According to Peattie (2001), the evolution of green marketing has three phases. First phase was termed as "Ecological" green marketing, during this period all marketing activities were concerned to help environment problems and provide remedies for environmental problems. Second phase was "Environmental" green marketing and the focus shifted on clean technology that involved designing of innovative new products, which take care of pollution and waste issues. Third phase was "Sustainable" green marketing. It came into prominence in the late 1990s and early 2000.

3.5. Concept of Green Marketing in Asia

The green issue is concerned by all communities throughout the world. Environmentally related issues such as air or water pollution, noise pollution, and the unexpected climate change, the ozone layer's problem and its undesirable effect on environment are quite well informed to individuals. In the recent times, consumers' concern toward environmental issues has become prominent where they realize that their purchase intention will be able to influence the environment. Asian region has also taken the responsibility to sustain the environment through embracing the power of "going-green". Due to fast-growing economy in Asia, the purchasing power of Asia has increased compared to previous generation. Many Asian countries have raised the environment awareness and they are willing to purchase the green product which has less harmful effect against environment.

Table 3.2: Social, Economic, and Environmental Dimensions of Seventeen Major Asian Countries

Stages of Development	Countries
Stage I	Vietnam, Lao PDR, India, Pakistan, Cambodia, Bangladesh and Myanmar
Transition from Stage I to II	Mongolia, Philippines, and Brunei Darussalam
Stage II	China, Thailand, and Indonesia
Transition from Stage II to III	Malaysia
Stage III	Singapore, Japan, and Republic of Korea

Source: Eun Kyung Jang, Mi Sun Park , Tae Woo Roh and Ki Joo Han (2015), Policy Instruments for Eco-Innovation in Asian Countries, Sustainability, Vol. 7, Pp. 12586-12614.

Table 3.3: Types of Policy Instruments

Stages of Development	Policy Instruments
Regulatory Instruments	Laws, Regulations, Orders and Decisions
Economic Instruments	Grants, Taxes, and Subsidies
Informational Instruments	Training, Forums, Conferences, Workshops, and Exhibitions
Planning Instruments	National Plans, Strategies, Programs, Actions and Roadmaps

Source: Eun Kyung Jang, Mi Sun Park , Tae Woo Roh and Ki Joo Han (2015), Policy Instruments for Eco-Innovation in Asian Countries, Sustainability, Vol. 7, Pp. 12586-12614

Eco-innovation policies in seventeen Asian countries were described with three public policy instruments: planning, regulatory, and economic. The sectors are subject to national plans and programmes as planning instruments, legislation as regulatory instruments, and financial mechanisms as economic instruments.

Most of the selected countries initiated national plans for green growth and innovation in the 2000s. National plans include several sectors that are related to eco-innovation, such as environmental protection, waste, renewable energy, purchase/procurement, clean technology, and climate change. However, Mongolia, Brunei Darussalam, and Myanmar have not yet initiated national plans that are directly related to eco-innovation. All target countries emphasized innovative green technologies in their national plans. Except for Brunei Darussalam, all countries introduced strategies for vitalizing renewable energy and mitigating and adapting to climate change. Several countries established policies for green purchasing or green procurement, which can be referred to as integrating environmental considerations into purchasing policies, programmes, and actions.

3.6. Green Consciousness among Indians in Traditional and Middle Era

Indian civilisation has been known as an 'eco-friendly' civilisation. At least in the past it did express a profound awareness of the need to evolve a balanced pattern in the man-environment interaction and certainly not work towards 'denaturing humanity.' In order to calibrate this man-environment interaction, ancient Indians divinized nature and laid down well formulated guidelines to define and nurture this relationship free of exploitative propensities.

The Rig-Veda establishes the symbolism of this close kinship when it says: 'Heaven is my father; my mother is this vast earth, my close kin.' Taking forward this environmental tradition the Atharva-Veda contains the hymn "Bhumi Sukta" ("earth clenching" in praise of the earth and invokes a balance: upon the immutable, vast earth supported by the law, the universal mother of the plants, peaceful and kind, may we ever walk for ever. The elaborate Vedic ritual of 'Athiratram' had, as its precise objective the generation of a positive impact on man and the environment and continues to be performed to this day with the same fervour and faith. Surapala's Vrikshāyurveda, for example, discusses in detail trees, tree planting and various other topics connected with plant-science including the treatment of sick-trees.

In one of its profound ecological perceptions the Mahabharata, in the Bhisma Parva, refers to the earth as an 'ever-yielding cow' provided its resources are developed and managed with balance and control: 'if Earth is well looked after, it becomes the father, mother, children, firmament and heaven, of all creatures.' The Mahabharata also compares the tree to the universe; it says that he who 'worships the ashvattha [peepal, holy fig tree] worships the universe.' The tree was seen as a symbolic representation of the universe with a single trunk and its multiple branches of manifestation. The Bodhi tree (ashvattha or peepal), under which the

Buddha achieved his realisation has been always seen as the symbol of 'the universal consciousness.' The wish-endowing symbol was that of the tree the kalpavriksha or kalpataru, the mystical tree that granted every wish just as nature showered its bounty on all. Tree worship, as findings reveal, was in fact known even in the Harappan culture. Trees and plants continue to play an important role in Indian rituals and customs to this day, especially in rural India.

This deep ecological consciousness pervaded the entire Indian civilisational mindscape and saw expressions from across the land. The legendary philosopher of Tamilakam, Thiruvalluvar, talks of nature as man's fortress. If he destroys her, he remains without protection. Even in the affairs of the state, the administration and the ruler were directed to preserve and promote environmental welfare. In the Arthasastra, Kautilya suggests the need to develop abhayāranya or abhayavana, forest and animal sanctuaries, where trees and animals would both dwell free from the fear of slaughter. Kautilya also prescribed the post of a forest superintendent and penalties for poaching and causing damage to forests, especially productive ones.

The sacred grove tradition was an intrinsic part of the Indian ecological imagination and tradition. There was the kovilkādu in Tamil Nadu, kāvu in Kerala, nandavana or daivavana in Karnataka and Andhra Pradesh, deorai in Maharashtra. Preserved for centuries in the outer precincts of the village these sacred groves gradually grew into rich ecological repositories and are facing threats of decimation today because of population pressure and neglect.

The Indian environmental tradition was conscious of the need to protect nature and to harness it within prescribed limits. Harappan sites at Dholavira, for example, demonstrate the elaborate techniques employed for water harvesting and storing. The initial structure of the Grand Anicut on the river Kaveri, erected by the great Chola King Karikala who ruled around 180 C.E. diverted the Kaveri waters without 'impounding them' and is believed to have irrigated 30,000 hectares during that period. Temple tanks served the dual purposes of 'ritual ablution' as well recharging of the groundwater level.

The Arthasastra's directives on water indicate that it was regarded as a 'collective, not a private commodity' and was considered extremely precious. Tanks were built through joint efforts of all stakeholders and the period that saw the construction or renovation of tanks received tax reprieves. Fines were also prescribed for a number of acts that adversely affected water bodies, 'for obstructing or diverting a water course', for 'damaging embankments' etc. The river in Indian civilisation was also endowed with divinity and was a cosmos by itself with ecological, social and spiritual dimensions. They were classified according to their sacredness and capacity to spiritually elevate man. The seven sacred rivers of India continue to remain a vibrant symbol signifying Indian civilisational continuity as well as unity. Like the sacred forests and groves, rivers too in the Indian context assured the seeker of spiritual height and perfection. Circumambulation of the river Narmada–a 2600 km route–was considered one of the most sacred acts in the Indian spiritual tradition. Rivers in the Indian tradition were not regarded as 'merely flowing mass of waters,' but rather as 'life-bestowing, life-nurturing, and life-protecting divine mothers.' The Satapatha-Brahmana and the Rig-Veda both abound in references to the sacredness of rivers and their organic link with man and his civilisation. Rivers were 'implored for protection'; were referred to as the very breath of the people, seen as the sources of plenitude and were prayed to for granting people 'nourishment and delight.' Venerated as divine beings they were treated with deference and sensitivity.

The situation is obviously different today. Pressures of modern life and an increasingly materialistic mode of living to a large extent served to sever these age-old eco-friendly links in India between man and his environment, especially, after the independence of the nation in 1947 followed by industrial revolution i.e. five-year plan periods.

3.7. Green Marketing in India in Modern Era

As stated above the concept of environmental protection has depilating among Indian since the beginning of industrial policy era in 1950. Rapid economic development and industrial growth resulted in high environment pollution of soil, earth, air and waters. All these pollutant factors are considered as the primary reason of the faster rising global warming status. Modern day consumers have started gaining more awareness about these environmental issues like global warming and the impact of environmental pollution. To overcome these issues of global warning and pollutions green marketing phenomenon has been developed. This phenomenon is particularly important in the modern market and has emerged as an important concept in India as in other parts of the developing and developed countries and is seen as an important strategy of facilitating sustainable development.

Though, green marketing is still in the nascent stage among the Indian companies, as of now in India, only around 25 per cent of the consumers prefer environmentally friendly products and appears that all types of consumers, both individual and industrial are becoming more concerned and aware about the natural environment. Lots of opportunities are available for green marketing in India. Consumers too are ready to pay premium price for green products in order to protect the mother earth. This transformation in consumer's behaviour is compelling the corporates to think about the harmful impact of their activities on the environment. The rapid increase for the environment concern in the last two decades is stressing companies to ensure the sustainable growth of the society. Marketers need to understand the implications of green marketing. They have to redraft their marketing practices and strategies in acceptance to green concepts. Successful marketing has to appeal to personal values of consumers and delivering consumer empowerment of right mix of marketing practices to harshness the competitive advantages.

3.8. Main Reasons for Adopting the Concept of Green Marketing by Indian Firms

Green marketing is also called environmental marketing/ecological marketing. As resources are limited and human wants are unlimited, it is important for the marketers to utilize the resources efficiently without waste as well as to achieve the organisation's objective. So green marketing is inevitable. There is growing interest among the consumers all over the world regarding the protection of the environment. Worldwide evidence indicates people are concerned about the environment and are changing their behaviour. As a result of this, green marketing has emerged which speaks for the growing market for sustainable and socially responsible products and services. Now this has become new mantra for marketers to satisfy the needs of consumers and earn better profits. The green marketing is implemented due to two force factors that is government pressure and CSR (Corporate Social Responsibility) of big corporate.

3.8.1 *Governmental Pressure*

In general, governments want to "protect" both consumers and marketers. For the same, Governmental regulations relating to environmental marketing are designed to protect overall environment in several ways:

- Reduction in the production of harmful goods or by-products.
- Modification in consumer and industry's use and or consumption of harmful goods.
- Ensuring that all types of consumers have the ability to evaluate the environmental composition of goods.

Governments in both developed and developing countries have regulated many by-products of production are controlled through the issuing of various environmental licenses. In some cases, the government's aim to "induce" final consumers to become more responsible. For example, some governments have introduced voluntary curb-side recycling programmes, making it easier for consumers to act responsibly. In other cases governments tax individuals who act in an irresponsible manner.

3.8.2 *Corporate Social Responsibility and Green Marketing*

CSR is a highly popularised agenda of many corporate bodies in today's competitive scenario. Not only big companies like Tata, Birla, and Reliance are associated for the social good in their operations, but also every well-established companies are also trying their best for the development of society and for the betterment of social set-up CSR, which is going good to society, always ensures the safety of the consumer which has a similar motive of using green product. CSR always aims to take precautionary step to protect all the environmental changes and also promote socio-economic rights of the consumers. It can be rightly claimed that implementation and enforcement of adopting the green concept is speeding up day by day and also the Indian government is installing economic stimulation to adopt environmental friendly measures.

3.9. Marketing Mix of Green Marketing

Green marketing mix is derived from the conventional marketing. It usually consists of four Ps, but every company adapts its favourite marketing mix. Thus the marketing mix is not limited to only four Ps, but can consist of other influencing factors as well. And there as 3Ps more that influence green marketing practices, namely people, planet and profits.

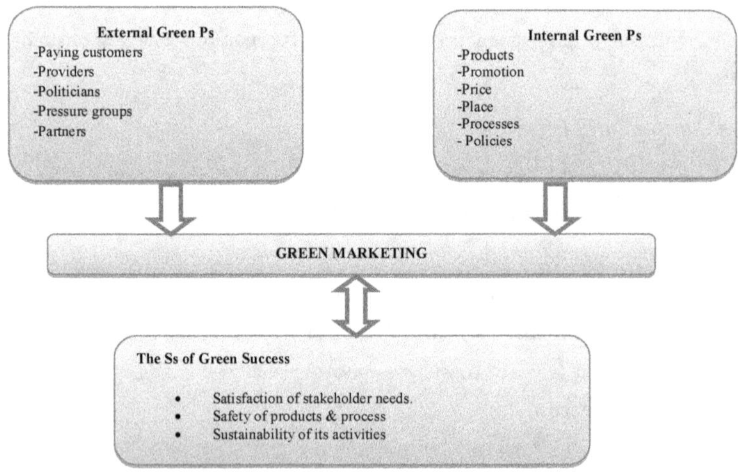

Exhibit 3.1: Green Marketing Process

Source: Shilpi Katiyar (2015), An Overview of Green Marketing for Indian Market, Abhinav National Monthly Refereed Journal of Research in Commerce and Management, Vol. 4, No. 2, Online ISSN-2277-1166, February.

- **Product:** Manufacturer of green products develops green products depending on the needs of the customers who prefer environment-friendly products. Products can be made from recycled materials or from used goods. Efficient products not only save water, energy and money, but also reduce harmful effects on the environment. Green chemistry forms the growing focus of product development. The marketer's role in product management includes providing product designers with market-driven trends and customer requests for green product attributes such as energy saving, organic, green chemicals, local sourcing, etc. For example, Nike is the first among the shoe companies to market itself as green.

- **Price:** Green pricing takes into consideration the people, planet and profit in a way that takes care of the health of employees and communities and ensures efficient productivity. Value of these company products can be added to it by changing its appearance, functionality and through customisation, etc. Wal-Mart unveiled its first recyclable cloth shopping bag. IKEA started charging consumers when they opted for plastic bags and encouraged people to shop using its "Big Blue Bag".

- **Place:** Green place is about managing logistics to cut down on transportation emissions, thereby in effect aiming at reducing the carbon footprint. For example, instead of marketing an imported mango juice in India it can be licensed for local production. This avoids shipping of the product from far away, thus reducing shipping cost and more importantly, the consequent carbon emission by the ships and other modes of transport.

- **Promotion:** Green promotion involves configuring the tools of promotion, such as advertising, marketing materials, signage, white papers, websites, videos and presentations by keeping people, planet and profits in mind. British petroleum (BP) displays gas station which is sunflower theme and boasts of putting money into solar power. Indian Tobacco Company has introduced environmentally-friendly papers and boards, which are free of elemental chlorine. Toyota is trying to push gas/electric hybrid technology into much of its product line. It is also making the single largest R&D (Research and Development) investment in the every-elusive hydrogen car and promoting itself as the first eco-friendly car company. International Business Machines Corporation (IBM) has revealed a portfolio of green retail store technologies and services to help retailers improve energy efficiency in their IT (Information Technology) operations.

- Green marketers can attract customers on the basis of their performance, money savings, health and convenience or by their environmental friendliness concepts to target a wide range of green consumers. Consumer awareness can be created by spreading the message among consumers about the benefits of environmentally-friendly products. Positing of profiles related to green marketing on social networks creates awareness within and across online peer groups. Marketing can also directly target the consumers through advertisements for product such as energy-saving compact fluorescent lamps, the battery powered Reva car, etc.

Table 3.4: SWOT Analysis of Green Marketing

Strengths	Weakness
<ul><li>Green Marketing builds brand equity and wins brand loyalty among customers.</li><li>Marketers can charge a premium on products that are seen as more eco-responsible.</li><li>Marketers get access to new markets and gain an advantage over competitors those who are not focusing on greenness.</li><li>Organisations that adopt green marketing are perceived to be more social responsibility.</li><li>It saves money in the long run, although initial cost is more e.g. research and development capabilities for clean processes and green products and human resources committed to environmental protection.</li></ul>	<ul><li>Overemphasizing greenness rather than customer needs can prove devastating for a product.</li><li>Many customers keep away from product labelled "Green" because they see such labelling as a marketing gimmick.</li><li>Most customers choose to satisfy their personal needs before caring for environment.</li><li>It will take a lot of time and effort for reaching green movement among consumers.</li><li>e.g. products cannot be recycled, and hazardous wastes of a company.</li></ul>
Opportunities	**Threats**
<ul><li>Organisations perceive Green Marketing to be a competitive advantage, relative to the competitors.</li><li>Marketing to segment which are becoming more environmentally aware and concerned. These consumers are demanding products that conform to these new attitudes.</li><li>Organisations perceive green marketing to be a competitive advantage, relative to the competitors. Firms, therefore, strive to improve upon their societal awareness. This complements the increase in consumers' socially conscious behaviour and will therefore give them an advantage over competitors who do not address these issues e.g. offering an environmentally-friendly product and saving resources, and relating them.</li></ul>	<ul><li>Uncertainty as to which Green Marketing activities are acceptable from a government perspective.</li><li>Uncertainty to the environment impact of present activities perceived to be less environmentally harmful.</li><li>Green marketing has to strive hard in convincing the stakeholders and many a times it may fail to convince them about the long-term benefits of Green marketing as compared to short-term expenses.</li><li>Indian literate and urban consumer is getting more aware about the merits of Green products. But it is still a new concept for the masses.</li><li>To face the marketing myopia e.g. competitors gain market shares with green products and increased environmental regulations.</li></ul>

Source: Saleena .TA (2015), SWOT Analysis of Green Marketing in India, EPRA International Journal of Economic and Business Review, Vol. 3, No. 12, e-ISSN: 2347-9671, p-ISSN: 2349-0187.

3.9.1   Green Products and Its Characteristics

The products that are manufactured through green technology and that caused no environmental hazards are called green products. Promotion of green technology and green products is necessary for conversation of natural resources and sustainable development. We can define green products by the following measures:-

Exhibit 3.2: Means of Identification of Green Products

Source: Pictogram Developed for the Study

Any product before reaching to the end-user goes through various stages of production and at each stage there is extensive use of resources like water, energy, fuel, etc. So, it becomes very important to optimize the use of these resources at every stage in order to mitigate the potential environmental impacts during the production phase. Not only during the production, but also during the use and after the disposal/end of life of the product, it can lead to major environmental hazards. In order to address these issues, a product is to be assessed based on its impacts on the environment at every stage of its life cycle from raw material extraction/procurement to its disposal/end of life. Sharma (2011) explained the four stages of green products:

Table 3.5: Stages of Green Products

Stage-1	**Development Stage:** Traditionally characterized as the acquisition of the raw materials, components parts and subassemblies. The alternative approach advocated here encourages manufacturer to check the environmental programme of suppliers, to acquire minimal packaging of input, and to consider sources of materials that could be easily replenished or are recyclable.
Stage-2	**Production Stage:** Manufacturing companies are encouraged to reduce emission, toxicity and waste, and to conserve water and energy. They are also to seek and develop alternative use of waste products, to revise the manufacturing process, to minimize waste generation, to minimize energy use or to attempt to find alternative sources of energy.
Stage-3	**Consumption Stage:** Minimization of packaging, conservation of energy and minimization of waste from product maintenance and service are strongly urged.
Stage-4	**Recycle Stage:** The final stage of product is its disposal, green marketing introduces the concepts of reuse and recyclability, in addition to the concept of waste reduction.

Source: Pawan Kumar (2015), Green marketing Products in India, DAV Academic Review A Refereed Research Journal, Vol.1, No.1.

From product life cycle concept, the cycle starts at the designing of product. Green design emphasises both environmentally conscious design and life cycle assessment/analysis. In designing a product, the designing team can change the raw materials or substances used during the manufacturing to be less toxic, more environmentally friendly.

3.9.2   *Nature of Green Products*

Green products can be described as the products that have qualities that protect environment and have replaced chemical ingredients with natural ingredients. These goods are produced with a least impact on environment in an energy-conservative manner or made from recycled components, without the use of chemicals that could harm both consumer and environment and these products are supplied to market with recyclable or less packing materials. Some categories of green products are presented in Table. 3.6.

Table 3.6: Features of Green Products

Product	Green Product	Green Features
Food	Organic Food	Produced using environmentally and animal friendly farming method on organic farms
Beverages	Organic winc	Produced from grapes through organic farming without use of chemical and pesticides
Textiles	Organic fiber	Produced from cotton, jute, silk or wool obtained from organic farm, free from genetically modified seeds, without use of harmful herbicides and pesticides
Automobiles	Hybrid vehicles, hydrogen fuelled, electronic vehicles	Low carbon emissions, follow euro-vi or California's Zero Emission vehicle standards causing less pollution
Electronics	Energy efficient products – CFL, LEDs, bulbs	Low power consumption and less release of gasses in electronics like television, refrigerator, etc.
Plastics	Bioplastics	Biodegradable, producing plastic bags and products with thickness above 20micron which is recyclable
Paints	Lead- free paints, paints with zero Volatile Organic Compounds (VOC)	Release low level toxins after application, chemical free
Perfumes	Eco-friendly perfumes	Without chlorofluorocarbons (CFCs) propellants, using hydrocarbons and nitrous oxide as propellants
FMCGs	Herbal soaps, cosmetics, shampoos, etc.	Without chemicals, artificial colours and compounds harming skin and complexion

Source: Padmaja PL and Krishna Mohan (2016), A Study on Consumer Perspective towards Green Products in Bengaluru City, India, Journal of Economics and Business Research, ISSN: 2068-3537, E-ISSN (online) 2069-9476, ISSN-L=2068-3537, Vol. 22, No. 1, Pp. 137-151.

As people all over the world become more aware about the importance of protecting the environment and using green products, the demand for them has become increasingly higher. Eco-friendly products, also known as *green products.* Green products stress the straight and tangible benefits provided by greener designs, such as energy efficiency or recycled content, rather than stressing the environmental attributes them. For Example, CNG (Converted Natural Gas) use in the vehicles, super concentrated laundry detergents not only save energy and packaging they save end space, money and effort. Therefore, Green product means any product, which is not hazardous for environment and customer as well, and it also works as a future remedy for negative impact of a product.

3.9.3   *Promotional Strategies for Green Products*

Among the most visible approaches of promoting green consumerism are eco-labelling schemes for products and services, public awareness campaigns, eco-efficient production standards and process certification (especially achieved through green technology), green public procurement by governments and public institutions, and recycling activities of post-use products. This is reflected in the works of international bodies such as the United Nations Environment Programme product labelling codes and standards, and waste recycling policies of national governments, Corporate Social Responsibility (CSR) strategies of companies; and shopping and or domestic waste recycling by households.

- "Eco Labelling" can assure the customer about the genuineness of the green product and can make it popular.
- Create consumer awareness about the big companies who have adopted the concept of green marketing or green product e.g.
- Nike is the first company in shoe making which is promoting and marketing its air Jordan shoes as environment-friendly, as they have reduced the usages of harmful glue and adhesive.
- Dell is using eco-friendly packaging with a system recycling kit with the IT product.
- SBI has also emerged into the concept of green services which is known as "Green Channel Counter". In this they are trying to focus on paper-less banking, no slip for deposition of money, no withdrawal forms, no cheques etc.
- Agartala is to be India's first Green City. All the public and private vehicles in Agartala run on Compressed Natural Gas (CNG) from 2013.
- Tata is also planning to setup an eco-friendly showroom using natural building material for its flooring and energy efficient lights.
- Eco Sponsoring: One of the most popular ways of promoting product is sponsoring which draws the attention very quickly and also cast a very strong impression in the mind of the consumer and somewhat it is also related with the reputation of the sponsor. Companies must engage themselves with the projects related with environmental or ecological issues. There are many other ideas also like involvement of the company into recycling programme, reuse programme, community services programme etc.

3.10. Understanding Green Consumers

Green consumerism refers to the production, promotion, and preferential consumption of goods and services on the basis of their pro-environment claims. The green consumers are the driving forces behind the green marketing process. Green consumers create demand for green products, which in turn encourages improvements in the environmental performance of many products and companies. Thus, for a marketer it is important to identify the types of green consumers. Many organisations have found that two out of every three consumers are green in developed countries, whereas, in developing countries like India and Bangladesh one out of every six consumers are green, but their environmental commitments vary because of their different standards, expectations from procedures, demand and buying power. Thus, it is not efficient to claim that the green consumers are those who engage in green consumption, especially, consumers in more sustainable socially responsible.

It is an undeniable fact that consumer appetite for green products has increased significantly in the past years. Now-a-days consumers are more choosy in their green choices especially while buying personal care, food and household products that directly affect them and their families. Moreover consumers in developing countries are expanding their green purchase interest to higher-ticket items such as cars and technology. However, consumers, in developing countries claim that green products have a higher inherent value. Ninety-five per cent of Chinese consumers say they are willing to spend more on a product because it is green with 55 per cent of them willing to spend between 11-30 per cent more. Similarly 29 per cent of Indian consumers and 48 per cent of Brazilians say they are willing to spend between 11-30 per cent more on green products. Similarly, consumers in developing countries express greater concern over the state of the environment in their countries, which may contribute to their greater willingness to pay more for green products. A great deal of market research has been concerned with identifying the green consumers. A clear picture has not yet been established and it differs a lot between markets. But some generalizations about the green consumers can be made on the basis of the research done so far. The Green Consumer: (i) Is Consistent (ii) Is Confused (iii) Is Generally a Woman and (iv) Is sophisticated in wants and needs.

3.11. Challenges of Green Marketing

Many organisations want to turn green, as an increasing number of consumers' want to associate themselves with environmentally-friendly products. Alongside, confusion has also been witnessed among the consumers regarding the products. In particular, a consumer often finds distrust regarding the credibility of green products. Therefore, to ensure consumer confidence, marketers of green products need to be much more transparent and refrain from breaching any law or standards relating to products or business practices.

In adopting green marketing policies, firms may encounter many challenges. Key green marketing challenges are as follows:

- **New Concept:** Green marketing is still a new concept in India. People living in rural areas still a lack of awareness regarding the benefits of green marketing. The consumer needs to be educated and made aware of the environmental threats. The new green movement needs to reach the masses and that will take a lot of time and effort. Now- a-days, Indian consumers do appreciate the importance of using natural and herbal beauty products through the knowledge transferred through India's Ayurvedic heritage. Indian consumer is exposed to healthy living lifestyle such as yoga and natural food consumption. These days consumers are ready and will be inclined to accept the green products.

- **Need for Equivalence:** Generally, it has been observed that very less percentage of the marketing messages and information is known from green campaigns and there is a lack of equivalence to validate these claims from the manufacturer's end point. There is no homogeneity to verify these claims. Recently, there is no consistency put to efforts made by them to declare officially a product as organic. Unless some regulatory bodies are involved in providing the certifications verification of green products are impossible. There is an urgent need for establishments of a standard quality control board for such labelling and licensing of green products.

- **Cost Factor:** Green products require renewable and recyclable material, which is costly. Further Green marketing involves marketing of green products/services, green technology, green power/energy for which requires a huge investment in R&D programmes for their development and subsequent promotional programmes which may ultimately lead to increased cost of green products, which consumers may find it very difficult to pay.

- **Information Disclosures:** The potential challenge in front of the corporate firms/ small retailers of green products is ensuring that information provided on greenness must be adequate and reliable. Secondly, that information should not be false unsubstantiated claims. On the other hand, it is the duty of central and state government to check whether these claims are permissible. Further, the government should establish eco-labels and fixed price mechanism which can serve as a useful measure for green marketing.

- **Endurance and Perseverance:** The investors and the corporates required viewing the environment as a chief long-term speculation opportunity to gaze at the long-term benefits from this new green movement. It will need a lot of persistence and it has no instantaneous results. Since it is a new concept and idea, it will have its own acceptance period. More promotions on green marketing practices have to make this concept very popular.

- **Convincing Customers:** Another major challenge for a firm is convincing the customers for selling their green products because the customers may not believe easily the firm's strategy of Green marketing, therefore many corporate firms are undertaking all possible measures to convince the customers about their green products.

- **Avoiding Green Myopia:** Another major challenge of green marketing is green myopia i.e., prejudice notion of consumers about green products. Misjudging or overemphasising the former at the expense of the latter can be termed-green marketing myopia i.e., non-conventional products against conventional products or vice-versa. The first rule of green marketing is focusing on customer benefits i.e., the primary reason why consumers buy certain products in the first place. Marketers of green products have to motivate their consumers to switch brand or even pay a premium for the greener products instead of buying a non-green products. This marketing practice cannot be pass to customer satisfaction criteria. This will lead to green myopia. For avoiding green marketing myopia, a marketer aims to fulfil consumers' needs and interests beyond environmental requirements.

- **Social Auditing of Green claims:** Another problem of green marketing is lack of adaptation of social auditing of the green claim. It is a generally accepted principle that the claims of the market and non-market forces of going green must be done only through proper auditing procedure but the reality is that there is no legal authority to verify or evaluate such claims. Moreover, if some political parties are not interested to implement environment protective measures. For example, some state governments tried and issued notification banning use of polythene bags, but in practice, it could not be controlled and the polythene bags are used openly in the market, which is against the environmental protection.

- **Sustainability:** Green Companies should realise the fact that initially the profits are very low since renewable and recyclable products and green technologies are more expensive. Green marketing will be successful only in the long run. Hence the business needs to plan for long- term rather than short-term strategy and prepare for the same, and at the same time it should avoid falling into the lure of unethical practices to make profits in the short run.

- **Non-Cooperation:** The firms practising green marketing have to strive hard in convincing the stakeholders and many a times it may fail to convince them about the long-term benefits of green marketing as compared to short-term expenses.

- **Unwilling to Pay Premium:** If green products are produced more, then the cost of production will rise due to the rise of raw material cost, and further after rise of production cost and low sales, the price of the green product will again rise. In that condition consumers are not ready to pay a premium amount for green products. It is always considered as an issue in marketing of green product.

3.12. Success of Green Marketing

To be a successful green marketing company there are a few fundamental rules that will go a long way in shaping the future of the business in the coming years. The fundamental strategy is to use the Four Ps suitably modified to meet the needs of Green Marketing, but there are a few points that are needed to be stressed before embarking on strategy. They are:

- **Knowing the Customer:** Marketers should ensure that the consumers are aware of and concerned about the issues that the product attempts to address, without which success in green marketing will be difficult to achieve.

- **Educating the Customer:** The marketers should educate their customers through advertisement and mouth-to-mouth canvassing about the benefits of using green products, and how it will reflect on the health of their family members as well as the health of the nation.

- **Genuineness and Transparency to the Customer:** It shows that **a)** In reality marketers should practise actually, what they can claim to be doing in their green marketing campaign and **b)** their business policies should be on a par with whatever they are doing in the name of eco-friendly activities. Both these conditions have to be met for their business to establish the kind of environmental credentials that will allow a green marketing campaign to succeed.

- **Reassuring the Buyer:** Marketers should ensure that the customers must be made to believe that the product being offered shall fulfil the objective or purpose for which it has been purchased i.e.no compromise in product quality in the name of the environment.

- **Pricing for the Customer:** Marketers should ensure that consumers can afford the premium and feel it is worth, which is being charged for their product, as many environmentally preferable products cost more due to economies of scale and use of higher-quality ingredients.

- **Giving the Customers an Opportunity to Participate**: Marketers should personalize the benefits of their environmentally friendly actions, normally through letting the customer take part in a positively environmental action, at same time keep in view the changed expectations of the customers.

3.13. Reasons for Companies Going Green

While looking through the literature there are several suggested reasons for firms increased use of green marketing. Five possible reasons cited are:

Opportunity: In India, around 25 per cent of the consumers prefer environmentally-friendly products and around 28 per cent of them may be considered health-conscious. Therefore, green marketers have to capitalize the perception of the consumers towards green products.

Governmental Pressure: Various regulations are framed by the government to protect consumers and the society at large. The Indian government too has developed a framework of legislations to reduce the production of harmful goods and by-products. These reduce the industry's production and consumer's consumption of harmful goods, including those detrimental to the environment, for example, the ban of plastic bags, prohibition of smoking in public areas etc.

Cost of Profit Issues: Firms may also use green marketing in an attempt to address cost or profit- related issues. Disposing of environmentally harmful by–products, such as polychlorinated biphenyl (PCB) contaminated oil are becoming increasingly costly and in some cases difficult. Therefore firms that can reduce harmful wastes may incur substantial cost savings. When attempting to minimise waste, firms are often forced to re-examine their production processes. In these cases they often develop more effective production processes that not only reduce waste, but also reduce the need for some raw material.

Competitive Pressure: Another major force in the environmental marketing area has been firms' desire to maintain their competitive position. In many cases firms observe competitors promoting their environmental behaviours and attempt to emulate this behaviour. In some instances this competitive pressure has caused an entire industry to modify and thus reduce its detrimental environmental behaviour.

3.14. Conclusion

The elaborate theoretical discussions provide an outer look on green or environmental marketing. It has been understood that green marketing consists of all activities designed to generate and facilitate any exchanges intended to satisfy human needs, such that satisfaction of these needs and wants occur, with minimal detrimental impact on the natural environment. Green marketing is marketing of products that are presumed to be environmentally safe. Thus green marketing incorporates a broad range of activities, including product modification, changes to the production process, packaging changes, as well as modifying advertising. Green marketing is gaining noteworthy attention from both marketers and consumers. Over the last decade concern for the environmental issues has been increasing due to increased media exposure, greater awareness of environmental pollutions, the impact of major industry disasters and the rise of activist groups on the environment. In the last decade, consumers have become more enlightened on environmental issues. Based on the elaborate theoretical discussion made in this chapter, analysis and interpretation of primary data collected were presented in the following Chapter IV.

References

[1] Pawan Kumar, "Green marketing Products in India, DAV Academic Review" A Refereed Research Journal, Vol. 1, No.1, Pp. 47-63, 2015.

[2] Faizan Zafar Sheikh, Ashfaq Ahmed Mirza, Anam Aftab and Bilal Asghar, "Consumer Green Behaviour toward Green Products and Green Purchase Decision", International Journal of Multidisciplinary Sciences and Engineering, Vol. 5, No. 9, Pp. 1-9, 2014.

[3] Meenakshi Verma and Anuj Verma, "Green Marketing–Strategy and Scope of Growth in Indian Market", International Journal of Rural Development and Management Studies, Vol. 5, No. 2, Pp. 423-430, 2011.

[4] Chan Yew Ling, "Consumers' purchase intention of green products: an investigation of the drivers and moderating variable", Elixir Marketing Mgmt, Vol. 57A, Pp. 14503-14509, 2013.

[5] Pavan Mishra and Payal Sharma, "Green Marketing in India: Emerging Opportunities and Challenges", Journal of Engineering, Science and Management Education, Vo. 3, Pp. 9-14, 2010.

[6] Collins Marfo Agyeman, "Consumers' Buying Behavior Towards Green Products: An Exploratory Study", International Journal of Management Research and Business Strategy, Vol. 3, No.1, Pp. 188-197, 2014.

[7]   K. Lohith Kumar, N. Soma Sekhar, B. Chandramohanreddy and G. Chandrasekhar, "Emerging Opportunities and Challenges in Green Marketing", 3rd International Conference on Recent Innovation in Science Engineering and Management, 2016.

[8]   Sonal Pareek Kaushik, Sonal Alvares, Romil Bajaj and Shweta Arora, "Communicating Green Products to Consumers in India to promote Sustainable Consumption and Production: Study based on the Consumer Perceptions of Green Products in India", A Research Project conducted by: Green Purchasing Network of India, 2014.

[9]   The National Geographic/GlobeScan Greendex findings result from an international consumer survey conducted between 12th March to 3rd May, 2012.

[10] Collins Marfo Agyeman, "Consumers' Buying Behavior towards Green Products: An Exploratory Study", International Journal of Management Research and Business Strategies, Vol. 3, No. 1, Pp. 188-197, 2014.

[11] Capturing the Green Advantage for Consumer Companies, The Boston Consultancy Group Report, https://www.bcg.com/documents/file15407.pdf.

[12] Mohammad Tariq Intezar and M. Yaseen Khan, "Effect of green products on consumer attitude–A sustainable approach", American Journal of Business, Economics and Management, Vol. 2, No. 6, Pp. 170-175, 2014.

[13] Ishaswini and Saroj Kumar Datta, "Pro-environmental Concern Influencing Green Buying: A Study on Indian Consumers", International Journal of Business and Management, Vol. 6, No. 6, Pp. 123-133, 2011.

[14] Jacob Cherian and Jolly Jacob, "Green Marketing: A Study of Consumers' Attitude towards Environment Friendly Products", Asian Social Science, Vol. 8, No. 12, Pp. 117-126, 2012.

[15] http://environmentalprofessionalsnetwork.com/a-few-good-reasons-to-use-eco-friendly-products-for-a-greener-home/

[16] What are Eco-Friendly Products?, http://www.conserve-energy-future.com/25-green-eco-friendly-products.php.

[17] Fabien Durif, Caroline Boivin and Charles Julien, "In search of a green product definition", Innovative Marketing, Vol. 6, No. 1, Pp. 25-33, 2010.

[18] Jaya Tiwari, "Green marketing in India: An Overview", IOSR Journal of Business and Management (IOSR-JBM), 2nd National conference on Value Based Management-Business for value or Values in Business, Institute of Management MET, Pp. 33-40, 2013.

[19] Vemuri Lakshmi Narayana & Dhinesh Babu, Green Marketing-New Hopes and Challenges, 2nd June, 2008. http://www.indianmba.com/Faculty_Column/FC832/fc832.html.

[20] Communicating Green Products to Consumers in India to promote Sustainable Consumption and Production-A Study based on the Consumer Perceptions of Green Products in India, A Research Project conducted by: Green Purchasing Network of India, 2014. http://switch-greenretail.in/publication/article-on-green-products/wppa_open/

[21] Mohd Nazri Mohd Noor, Md Shukor Masuod, Al-Mansor Abu Said, Izzat Fakhruddin Kamaruzaman and Mohd Ariff Mustafa, "Understanding Consumer s and Green Product Purchase Decision in Malaysia: A Structural Equation Modeling-Partial Least Square (SEM-PLS)", Approach, Published by Canadian Center of Science and Education, Asian Social Science, Vol. 12, No. 9, Pp. 51-64, 2016.

[22] D. Mebratu, "Environmental competitiveness: Green purchasing", International Trade Forum, Vol.2, Pp. 11-13, 2001.

[23] M.I. Dantas, V.P. Minim, R. Deliza and R. Puschman, "The Effect of Packaging on the Perception of Minimally Processed Products", Journal of International Food and Agribusiness Marketing, Vol. 16, No. 2, Pp. 71-83, 2004.

[24] C. Gurau and A. Ranchhod, "International green marketing: a comparative study of British and Romanian firms", International Marketing Review, Vol. 22, No. 5, Pp. 547-561, 2005.

[25] Gan Christopher Han Yen Wee, Lucie Ozanne and Tzu-Hui Kao, "Consumers' purchasing behavior towards green products in New Zealand", Innovative Marketing, Vol. 4, No. 1, Pp. 93-102, 2008.

[26] OECD, "Sustainable Manufacturing and Eco-innovation: Towards a Green Economy, Policy Brief", 2009.

[27] Nurse Gretchen, Yuko Onozaka and Dawn Thilmany McFadden, "Understanding the Connections between Consumer Motivations and Buying Behavior: The Case of the Local Food System Movement", Presented in a Conference at the Southern Agricultural Economics Association Annual Meeting, Orlando, 2010.

[28] P.S. Pavan Mishra, "Golden Rule of Green Marketing", Green Marketing In India: Emerging Opportunities and Challenges, Vol. 3, No. 6, 2010.

[29] P.L. Peter, "The Willingness to Pay for Green and Fair Trade Product Types", Master Thesis, Erasmus University, Rotterdam, 2011.

[30] V. Mohanasundram, "Green Marketing-Challenges and Opportunities", International Journal of Multidisciplinary, Vol. 2, No. 4, Pp. 66-73, 2012.

[31] Subooh Yusuf and Zeenat Fatima, "Consumer Attitude and Perception towards Green Products", The International Journal of Indian Psychology, Vol. 2, No. 3, 2015.

[32] P.L. Padmaja and V. Krishna Mohan, "A study on Consumer Perspective towards Green Products in Bengaluru City, India", Journal of Economics and Business Research, Vol. 22, No. 1, Pp. 137-151, 2016.

[33] K. Peattie, "Towards sustainability: The third age of green marketing", The Marketing Review, Vol. 2, No. 2, Pp. 129-146, 2001.

[34] M. Ginsberg and N. Bloom, "Choosing the Right Green-Marketing Strategy", MIT Sloan Management Review, Vol. 46, No.1, Pp. 79-88, 2004.

[35] C. D'Souza, "Green advertising effects on attitude and choice of advertising themes", Asia Pacific Journal of Marketing and Logistics, Vol. 17, No. 3, Pp. 51-66, 2005.

[36] J.A. Ottman, "Avoiding green marketing myopia", Journal of Environment Review, Vol. 48, No. 5, Pp. 22-36, 2006.

[37] V. Soonthonsmai, "Environmental or green marketing as global competitive edge: Concept, synthesis, and implication", EABR (Business) and ETLC (Teaching) Conference Proceeding, Venice, Italy, 2007.

[38] Ravindra P. Saxena and Pradeep K. Khandelwal, "Consumer attitude towards green marketing: an exploratory study", University of Wollongong Research Online, 2008.

[39] B. Dutta, "Sustainable Green Marketing the New Imperative", Marketing Mastermind, The ICFA University Press, Hyderabad, Pp. 23-26, 2008.

[40] R. Shrikanth and D. Surya Narayana Raju, "Contemporary Green Marketing - Brief Reference to Indian Scenario", International Journal of Social Sciences & Interdisciplinary Research, Vol. 1, No.1, Pp. 26-39, 2012.

[41] G. Manjunath and Gundupagi Manjunath, "Green marketing and its implementation in Indian Business organizations", Asia Pacific Journal of Marketing & Management Review, Vol. 2, No.7, Pp. 75-86, 2013.

[42] Mohammad Azam, "Green Marketing: "Eco-Friendly Approach", International Journal of Innovative Research and Development, Vol. 3, No. 2, Pp. 78-80, 2014.

[43] Vishnu Nath, Rajat Agrawal, Aditya Gautam and Vinay Sharma ",Green marketing promotion tools and Indian consumers' green purchase intentions", Int. J. of Business Competition and Growth, Vol. 3, No. 4, Pp. 275–291, 2014.

[44] C. Dilip Kumar and S.M. Yamuna, "A Study on Consumer Preference towards Green Marketing Products", International Journal of Scientific Research, Vol. 3, No. 2, 2014.

[45] Anoop Kumar Singh and Shreyanshu Singh, "Green Marketing: Need of the Hour for Sustainable Development", International Journal of Social Relevance and Concern (IJSRC), Vol. 3, No. 6, Pp. 27-32, 2015.

[46] J. Karna, E. Hansen and H. Juslin, "Social Responsibility in Environmental Marketing Planning", European Journal of Marketing, Vol. 37, No. 5/6, Pp. 848-873, 2003.

[47] Pavan Mishra and Payal Sharma, "Green Marketing in India: Emerging Opportunities and Challenges", Journal of Engineering, Science and Management Education, Vol. 3, Pp. 9-14, 2010.

[48] G. Unruh and R. Ettenson, "Growing Green; Three smart paths to developing sustainable products", Harvard Business Review, Boston, Vol. 5, No. 6, 2010.

[49] K.P.V. Ramanakumar, C.G. Manojkrishnan and S.R. Suma, "Consumer Attitude towards Green Products of FMCG Sector: An Empirical Study", International Journal of Research in Commerce & Management, Vol. 3, No. 2, Pp. 34-38, 2012.

[50] R. Kumar, "Green marketing-A Brief Reference to India", Asian Journal of Multidisciplinary Studies, Vol. 1, No. 4, Pp. 191-203, 2013.

[51] Rajeev Kumar, "Green Marketing: The Next Big Thing", Journal of Sales and Marketing Management (JSMM), Vol. 2, No. 2, Pp. 9-14, 2015.

[52] M. Laroche, J. Bergeron, M. Tomiul and G. Barbaro-Forleo, "Cultural differences in environmental knowledge, attitudes and behaviours of Canadian consumers", Canadian Journal of Administrative Sciences, Vol. 19, No. 3, Pp. 267-283, 2002.

[53] C. Leire and A. Thidell, "Product-related environmental information to guide consumer purchases a review and analysis of research on perceptions, understanding and use among Nordic consumers", Journal of Cleaner Production, Vol. 13, No. 10, Pp. 61-70, 2005.

[54] C. D'Souza, M. Taghian, P. Lamb and R. Peretiatkos, "Green products and corporate strategy: An empirical investigation", Society and Business Review, Vol. 1, No. 2, Pp. 144-157, 2006.

[55] Krishna Kumar Veluri, "Green Marketing: Indian Consumer Awareness and Marketing Influence on Buying Decision", International Journal of Research In Commerce and Management, Vol. 3, No. 2, Pp. 60-66, 2012.

[56] Norazah Mohd. Suki, "Green awareness effects on consumers' purchasing decision: some insights From Malaysia", IJAPS, Vol. 9, No. 2, Pp. 1311-1319, 2013.

[57] Shruti P. Maheshwari, "Awareness of Green Marketing and its Influence on Buying Behaviour of Consumers: Special Reference to Madhya Pradesh, India", AIMA Journal of Management & Research, Vol. 8, No. 1/4, Pp. 1-14, 2014.

[58] Subooh Yusuf and Zeenat Fatima, "Consumer Attitude and Perception towards Green Products", The International Journal of Indian Psychology, Vol. 2, No. 3, 2015.

[59] Meghna Sharma & Prachi Trivedi, "Various Green Marketing Variables and their Effects on Consumers" Buying Behaviour for Green Products", IJLTEMAS, Vol. 5, No. 1, Pp. 1-8, 2016.

[60] A. Kollmuss and J. Agyeman, "Mind the gap: why do people act environmentally and what are the barriers to pro-environmental behavior?", Environmental Education Research, Vol.8, Pp. 239-260, 2002.

[61] M.M. Mostafa, "Gender differences in Egyptian consumers' green purchase behavior: the effects of environmental knowledge, concern and attitude, Hong Kong adolescent consumers' green purchasing behavior", Kaman Lee Journal of Consumer Marketing, Vol. 26, 2007.

[62] Dharmendra Mehta, Naveen K. Mehta and Sangeeta Jain, "Impact of Gender on Adolescent Consumers' towards Green Products (A Study Conducted in Indore City)", The Annals of The "Ştefan, 2011.

[63] Cel Mare, "Fascicle of The Faculty of Economics and Public Administration", Vol. 11, No. 1(13), Pp. 98-102.

[64] Sachin S. Vernekar and Preeti Wadhwa, "Green Consumption: An Empirical Study of Consumers Attitudes and Perception regarding Eco-Friendly FMCG Products, with special reference to Delhi and NCR Region", Opinion, Vol. 1, No. 1, Pp. 65-74, 2011.

[65] N. Mahesh, "Consumer's Perceived Value, Attitude and Purchase Intention of Green Products", SMS Varanasi, Vol. 9, No. 1, Pp. 36-43, 2013.

[66] Collins Marfo Agyeman, "Consumers' Buying Behavior towards Green Products: An Exploratory Study", International Journal of Management Research and Business Strategies, Vol. 3, No. 1, Pp. 188-197, 2014.

[67] B. Nagaraju and H. Thejaswini, "Consumers perception analysis-Market awareness towards eco-friendly FMCG products-A case study of Mysore district", IOSR Journal of Business and Management (IOSR-JBM), Vol. 16, No. 4, Pp. 64-71, 2014.

[68] Shweta Singh, Deepak Singh and K.S. Thakur, "Consumer's Attitude and Purchase Intention towards Green Products in the FMCG Sector", Pacific Business Review International, Vol. 7, No. 6, 2014.

[69] Muhammed Abdullah Sharaf, Filzah Md Isa and Khalid Al-Qasa, "Young Consumers' Intention towards Future Green Purchasing in Malaysia", Journal of Management Research, Vol. 7, No. 2, 2015.

[70] V. Ranganathan and S. Ramya, "A Study on Consumers' perception Towards Green Products with Reference to Coimbatore City", Imperial Journal of Interdisciplinary Research (IJIR), Vol. 2, No.2, Pp. 145-150, 2016.

[71] Sangeeta Gupta, Shallu and Mansi Kapoor, "A Study of Consumer Attitude and Awareness towards Green Marketing and Green Branding", Indian Journal of Applied Research, Vol. 4, No. 1, Pp. 315-319, 2014.

[72] K. Lohith Kumar, N. Soma Sekhar, B. Chandramohanreddy and G. Chandrasekhar, "Emerging Opportunities and Challenges in Green Marketing", 3rd International Conference on Recent Innovation in Science Engineering and Management (ICRISEM-16), Pp. 1097-1102, 2016.

[73] P. Alamelu Mangai and K. Subramaniam, "Efficacy of Green Marketing on Refinement of Indian Companies", International Journal of Marketing, Financial Services & Management Research, Vol. 6, No. 2, Pp. 35-45, 2017.

[74] A. Muthukumaran, "Emerging Strategies of Green Marketing in India", International Journal of Applied Research, Vol. 1, No. 10, Pp. 553-556, 2015.

[75] Govind Teju Rathod, "Green Marketing in India: Emerging Opportunities and Challenge", Asian Journal of Management Sciences, Vol. 2, No. 3, Pp. 111-115, 2014.

[76] Artee Aggrawal, "Factors Affecting Green Marketing In India: A Study of Metro Consumers", Factors Affecting Green Marketing In India-A Study of Metro Consumers Artee Agarwal.pdf, Pp. 32-34, 2010.

[77] V.N. Francis Wong, Lee Mei Yean, Lin Xin Ru and Low Siok Yin, "A Study on the Youth Attitudes toward Purchase Green Products in Malaysia and Singapore", A research project submitted in partial fulfillment of the requirement for the degree of Bachelor of International Business (HONS), Universiti Tunku Abdul Rahman, Faculty of Accountancy and Management, Department of International Business, 2012.

[78] T. Russel, "Introduction: In Greener Purchasing: Opportunities and Innovations", Greenleaf Publishing: Sheffield, UK.

[79] Anirban Ganguly , "Man and Environment in India: Past Traditions and Present Challenges",http://www.vifindia.org/article/2012/july/26/man-and-environment-in-india-past-traditions-and-present-challenges, 2012.

[80] Pawan Kumar, "Green marketing Products in India, DAV Academic Review", A Refereed Research Journal, Vol. 1, No. 1, Pp. 58-59, 2015.

[81] Priti Aggarwal, "Green Marketing in India: Emerging Opportunities and Challenges", Global Journal of Commerce and Management Perspective, Vol. 2, No. 4, Pp. 85-88, 2013.

[82] Pawan Kumar, "Green marketing Products in India", DAV Academic Review, A Refereed Research Journal, Vol. 1, No. 1, Pp. 58-59, 2015.

[83] Jaya Tiwari, "Green marketing in India: An Overview", IOSR Journal of Business and Management (IOSR-JBM), 2nd National conference on Value Based Management-Business for value or Values in Business, Institute of Management MET, Pp. 33-40, 2013.

[84] Swati Agarwal, "Green Marketing in India in 21st Century-Role and Opportunities", International Journal of Education and Science Research Review, Vol. 1, No. 2, Pp. 189-190, 2014.

[85] Ivan Kontic and Jasmin Biljeskovic, "Greening the marketing mix–A case study of the Rockwool Group", Thesis submitted to the Jonkoping International Business School, Jonkoping University of the Partial completion of Bachelor's Degree in Business Administration, 2010.

[86] http://gpnindia.org/green-products/

[87] Palanivel Subramaniyam, Karthick Srinivasan and Muni Prabaharan, "Approach for Green Product Design", International Journal of Innovation, Management and Technology, Vol. 2, No. 3, Pp. 244-248, 2011.

[88] The Importance of Eco-Friendly Products, http://jcrsupply.com/blog/the-importance-of-ecofriendly-products/, 2015.

[89] Akenji Lewis, Hotta Yasuhiko, Bengtsson Magnus and Hayashi Shiko, "EPR policies for electronics in developing Asia: an adapted phase-in approach", Waste Management and Research, Vol. 29, Pp. 919-930, 2011.

[90] Ibid., Lewis Akenji (2012).

[91] Consumer interest in green products expands across categories http://www.cohnwolfe.com/en/news/consumer-interest-green-products-expands-across-categories.

[92] Shilpi Katiyar, "An Overview of Green Marketing for Indian Market", Abhinav National Monthly Refereed Journal of Research in Commerce and Management, Vol. 4, No. 2, 2015.

[93] Parag Shil, "Evolution and Future of Environmental Marketing", Asia Pacific Journal of Marketing & Management Review Vol.1, No. 3, Pp. 76-79, 2012.

[94] R. Shrikanth and Surya D. Narayana Raju, "Contemporary Green Marketing-Brief Reference To Indian Scenario", International Journal of Social Sciences and Interdisciplinary Research, Vol. 1, No. 1, Pp. 29-31, 2012.

[95] N. Mahesh, "Consumer's Perceived Value, Attitude and Purchase Intention of Green Products", SMS Varanasi, Vol. 9, No. 1, Pp. 36-43, 2013.

[96] Parag Shil, "Evolution and Future of Environmental Marketing", IRJC Asia Pacific Journal of Marketing & Management Review, Vol. 1, No. 3, Pp. 74-81, 2012.

CHAPTER IV

ANALYSIS AND INTERPRETATION

4.1.   Introduction

Green is slowly and steadily becoming the symbolic colour of eco-consciousness in India. The growing consumer awareness about the origin of products and the concern over impending global environmental crisis are increasing the opportunities to marketers to convince consumers. Certain studies conducted in the past have commented that the Indian consumers possess environmental consciousness and are concerned for environmental protection. They actively support the environment by purchasing and consuming products which are known to be environmentally friendly. Also, they derive individual and social meaning in their environmentally favourable activities and are willing to adopt environmentally friendly lifestyle. This behavioural shift influences the Indian consumers' purchase decisions for green products. In the process of buying green products the consumers make attempts to learn about green products, gain green product-related knowledge and experience themselves in their purchase behaviours. Drawing evidences from the above discussion this analytical chapter aims to analyse the consumers' attitude, preferences and buying practices towards green products in Coimbatore City.

4.1.1.   *Demographic and Socio-economic Status of the Consumers*

Demographic variables such as age, sex, generally influence consumers' beliefs, attitudes or buying behaviour of green products directly. Moreover, many researchers have attempted to identify green consumers' profiles with an intention to characterize green market segments using demographic variables. This section of the study draws a clear understanding on the demographic and socio-economic status of the green products consumers surveyed in Coimbatore city, the elaborate data discussion is made in the Table 4.1 to 4.9.

Table 4.1: Gender of the Respondents

Sl. No	Gender	No. of Respondents	Percentage
1.	Male	338	45.07
2.	Female	412	54.93
	Total	750	100

From the above data table it has been inferred that majority i.e., 54.93 per cent of the respondents are female and the remaining 45.07 per cent of the respondents surveyed are male.

Hence it has been concluded that 54.93 per cent of the respondents surveyed are female. In most of the nuclear families female members of the family take the major decision of buying the FMCG goods that is required for the family need, this may be the reason that majority of the sample participants are observed to be women.

Table 4.2: Age of the Respondents

Sl. No	Age	No. of Respondents	Percentage
1.	25-30 Years	218	29.07
2.	31-35 Years	195	26.00
3.	36-40 Years	199	26.53
4.	41 Years & Above	138	18.40
	Total	750	100

Source: Primary Data

From the above data analysis it has been inferred that 29.07 per cent of the respondents are in the age group of 25-30 years. 26.53 per cent of the respondents are aged between 36-40 years. 26 per cent of the respondents are aged between 31-35 years. The remaining 18.40 per cent of the respondents are found to be in the age group of 41 years and above.

Hence it has been concluded that 29.07 per cent of the respondents are in the age group of 25-30 years. The study observed that majority of green product consumers are very young.

Table 4.3: Educational Qualifiaction of the Respondents

Sl. No	Educational Qualification	No. of Respondents	Percentage
1.	School Level	198	26.40
2.	UG	231	30.80
3.	PG	152	20.27
4.	Others	169	22.53
	Total	750	100

Source: Primary Data

From the above presented data it has been inferred that 30.80 per cent of the respondents have completed UG degree. 26.40 per cent of the respondents have completed school level education.

Further, 22.53 per cent of the respondents have acquired knowledge in various vocational and art/culture skill courses and the remaining 20.27 per cent respondents have said that they have completed PG degree

It has been concluded that 30.80 per cent of the respondents have completed UG degree. The study indicates that educated people are more mindful of environmental issues and its protection.

Table 4.4: Marital Status of the Respondents

Sl. No	Marital Status	No. of Respondents	Percentage
1.	Married	588	78.40
2.	Unmarried	161	21.47
3.	Others	1	0.13
	Total	750	100

Source: Primary Data

From the above data analysis it has been inferred that majority (78.40 per cent) of the respondents are married. 21.47 per cent of the respondents are unmarried and the remaining 0.13per cent of the respondents belong to "others" category.

The study found that majority (78.40 per cent) of the respondents is married.

Table 4.5: Occupation of the Respondents

Sl. No	Occupation	No. of Respondents	Percentage
1.	Agriculturist	103	13.73
2.	Self – Employed	186	24.80
3.	Professional	157	20.93
4.	Employee	146	19.47
5.	Others	158	21.07
	Total	750	100

Source: Primary Data

The above table depicts the occupational status of the respondents surveyed. It has been observed that out of 750 consumers surveyed, 24.80 per cent of the respondents are self-employed individuals and 21.07 per cent of them are engaged in other occupations in unorganized sectors. And 20.93 per cent of them are observed to be qualified professionals in their respective discipline like teaching, medical practices, auditing, engineering etc. 19.47 per cent of consumers are working in private and public sector organization. The remaining 13.73 per cent of the respondents are categorized as agriculturists.

Hence it has been concluded that 24.80 per cent of the respondents are self-employed entrepreneurs.

Table 4.6: Monthly Income of the Respondents

Sl. No	Monthly Income	No. of Respondents	Percentage
1.	Less than ₹.10.000	292	38.93
2.	₹.10,001 to ₹20,000	194	25.87
3.	₹.20,001 to ₹.30,000	181	24.13
4.	₹.30,001 to ₹.40,000	82	10.93
5.	₹.40,001 & Above	1	0.13
	Total	750	100

Source: Primary Data

From the above data analysis it has been observed that 38.93 per cent of the respondents monthly income falls below ₹.10000. 25.87 per cent of the respondents earning ranges between ₹.10001-₹.20000 and 24.13 per cent of the respondents earn between ₹.20001-₹.30000 per month. A batch of 10.93 per cent of the respondents earn between ₹.30,001-₹.40,000 per month. Further it has been observed that0.13 per cent of the respondents monthly earning falls in the category of ₹.40000 and above.

It is evident from the above data analysis that the consumers in the income bracket of ₹.10001- ₹.40000 prefer buying green products.

Table 4.7: Family Type of the Respondents

Sl. No	Type of Family	No. of Respondents	Percentage
1.	Joint	358	47.73
2.	Nuclear	392	52.27
	Total	750	100

Source: Primary Data

The above table indicates that out of 750 respondents surveyed, 52.27 per cent of the respondents live in nuclear family set-up. The remaining 47.73 per cent of respondents form a part of joint family.

Hence it has been clearly understood that 52.27 per cent of the respondents live in nuclear family set-up. As discussed in Table: 4.3 educational qualification of consumers is likely to increase their sensitivity to social and environmental problems. Thus, it can be rightly claimed that consumers with high or medium income bracket and with higher educational qualifications are more likely to be environmentally conscious than the below average and very high income consumers.

Table 4.8: Number of Members in the Family of the Respondents

Sl. No	Number of Members	No. of Respondents	Percentage
1.	2 Members	76	10.13
2.	3 Members	128	17.07
3.	4 Members	333	44.40
4.	Above 4 Members	213	28.40
	Total	750	100

Source: Primary Data

From the above data information it has been concluded that 44.40 per cent of the respondents have four members in their family. 28.40 per cent of the respondents have more than four members in their family. Further it has been observed that 17.07 per cent of the respondents families have three members and 10.13 per cent of the respondents families have two members.

It has been evidenced from the study that 44.40 per cent of the respondents have four members in their family. It is the normal size of nuclear modern Indian families that has a father, mother and two children in most of the case.

Table 4.9: Number of Earning Members in the Family

Sl. No	Earning Members	No. of Respondents	Percentage
1.	Single Income	364	48.53
2.	Dual Income	386	51.47
	Total	750	100

Source: Primary Data

The above table indicates that 51.47 per cent of the respondents have said that their family enjoys dual income benefits. Whereas, 48.53 per cent of the green consumers have said that they have single income source for running their family.

The study found that 51.47 per cent of the respondents surveyed belong to dual income family category.

Dual income status of the family can be considered as an important determinant for consuming green products in most of the urban cities.

4.1.2. *Consumers' Awareness about Green Products*

Consumer's awareness about green products is important for marketers and other stakeholders in understanding the green consumers' purchasing behaviour. Consumers' awareness and motivation continue to drive change in the marketplace, notably through the introduction of more green products. The growing consumer awareness about the origin of green products and the concern over impending global environmental crisis are increasing the opportunities to marketers to convince the consumers to buy green products more and more, at the same time the marketers should focus their attention on innovation and reintroduction of various green products.

This section of the study draws a detailed analysis on the consumers' awareness towards green products in Coimbatore city.

Moreover, from marketers' point of view knowledge of the consumer is fundamental in the development of marketing strategy.

Awareness of environmentally friendly products is recognized in most consumers' behaviour research as a characteristic that influences decision process. Consumer's awareness is a significant construct affecting how consumers collect and interpret information. Data discussion made in Table 4.10 to 4.14 focus on these issues of consumers' awareness towards green products.

Table 4.10: Consumers' Level of Awareness Towards Green Products

Sl. No	Awareness	No. of Respondents	Percentage
1.	Very High	124	16.53
2.	High	199	26.53
3.	Moderate	270	36.00
4.	Low	138	18.40
5.	Very Low	19	2.53
	Total	750	100

Source: Primary Data

The data presented in the above table clearly indicates that 36 per cent of the respondents have moderate level of awareness towards use of green products. 26.53 per cent of the respondents have high level of awareness about green products.

Similarly 18.40 per cent of the respondents have said that they have gained low level of awareness towards green products. On the contrary, it was observed that 16.53 per cent of the respondents have very high level of awareness about the green products and the remaining 2.53 per cent of the respondents have very low level of awareness towards green products.

It has been concluded that 36 per cent of the respondents have moderate level of awareness towards use of green products.

The study reveals that cconsumers' awareness towards green products is more associated with the individuals, values towards environment, social responsibility and ethical consciousness etc.

Many of the marketing studies conducted in the past have acknowledged the fact that the consumers' awareness about green marketing is directly influenced by their demographic and socio-economic status.

The consumers' understanding on the concept of green marketing differs between the consumers of developing countries and developed countries. Drawing the required evidences from the above discussion the following hypothesis is framed and tested.

H1: There exists a close association between consumers' level of awareness towards green products and their demographic and socio-economic status.

Table 4.11: Association Between Consumers' Level of Awareness About Green Products and Their Demographic & Socio- Economic Status

Variables		Mean	SD	F	Sig
Gender	Male	2.58	1.171	1.723	.190
	Female	2.68	.920		
Age	25 -30years	2.21	1.055	33.979	.000
	31-35 years	2.57	.908		
	36-40 years	2.75	.931		
	Above 40 years	3.26	1.013		
Marital Status	Married	2.64	1.041	2.894	.050
	Unmarried	2.51	.971		
	Others	1.00	-		
Educational Qualification	School level	2.86	1.271	33.630	.000
	UG	3.02	.860		
	PG	2.19	.638		
	Others	2.27	.991		
Occupation	Agriculturist	2.48	1.356	2.565	.037
	Self-employed	2.77	1.068		
	Professional	2.48	.867		
	Employee	2.71	1.244		
	Others	2.69	.617		
Monthly Income	Less than ₹.10000	2.76	.917	4.832	.001
	₹.10001 to ₹.20000	2.39	1.271		
	₹.20001 to ₹.30000	2.61	.903		
	₹.30001 to ₹.40000	2.84	1.036		
	Above ₹.40000	3.00	.		
Nature of Family	Joint	2.66	1.084	.261	.610
	Nuclear	2.62	1.001		
Family Members	2 members	1.67	.985	52.542	.000
	3 members	2.16	.934		
	4 members	2.80	.741		
	Above 4 members	3.03	1.197		
Earning Income	Single Income	3.06	1.032	137.334	.000
	Dual Income	2.24	.881		

Level of Significance: 5 per cent

The descriptive data analysis presented above states that women are more conscious in gaining more awareness about green products. Similarly, the adults at the age of 40 years, married and settled, with high income, mostly self-employed, having large families with single income earners in the family are more attentive in gaining information on green products or say eco-friendly products.

From the above table it has been inferred that probability value of ANOVA at 5 per cent level does establish a good relationship between the variables tested. Therefore, the hypothesis framed stands accepted and it has been concluded that there is an association between consumers' level of awareness about green products and their demographic and socio- economic status. The empirical findings declared in this section of the study finds its relevance with the conclusion drawn by earlier researchers Mahesh (2013) and Mostafa (2007). Mahesh (2013) had claimed in his study that the middle-aged consumers and employees of private sector have more perceived value towards green products. The majority of the consumers are more concerned with their food safety, the protection of the environment and animal welfare. The consumers who have higher education levels and higher monthly income are more likely to purchase green products. The study found that the middle-aged consumers and employees of private sector have more intention in purchasing of green products. Similarly, Mostafa (2007) had confirmed in his study that gender does not influence the consumers' buying behaviour towards green products. Moreover, the study of Mclntyre Meleche and Lewis (1993) revealed that females were more conscious than their male counterparts, especially with reference to eco-friendly green products.

Table 4.12: Consumers' Opinion on Sources of Information on Green Products

Sl. No	Source of Information	No. of Respondents (N=3373)	Proportionate Percentage
1.	Television Commercials	489	65.20
2.	Radio Programmes /Commercials	551	73.47
3.	Newspapers	610	81.33
4.	Magazines	527	70.27
5.	Trade Fairs	463	61.73
6.	Others	733	97.73

Source: Primary Data

From the above table it has been clearly inferred that 97.73 per cent of the respondents have sourced information about green products from yoga class, art of living class, seminars, public gathering and from other naturopathy classes etc. Whereas, 81.33 per cent of the respondents have sourced information from the newspapers. Similarly 73.47 per cent of the respondents have gained information about green products from the radio programmes or commercials and 70.27 per cent of the respondents have gained information from the magazines. And 65.20 per cent of the respondents have sourced information through television commercials. Further it has been inferred that 61.73 per cent of the respondents have sourced information from trade fairs and exhibition stalls.

Thus it has been concluded that 97.73 per cent of the respondents have sourced information about green products from yoga class, art of living class, seminars, public gathering and from other naturopathy classes etc. The study has found that mass events and public programmes can contribute decisively to the formation of green product buying behaviour.

Table 4.13: Consumers' Opinion on Parameters Considered for Identification of Green Products

Sl. No	Parameters	No. of Respondents (N=4503)	Proportionate Percentage
1.	Products that are originally (naturally) grown	464	61.87
2.	Products that save energy	422	56.27
3.	Products that are recyclable, reusable and biodegradable	482	64.27
4.	Products with natural ingredients	583	77.73
5.	Products containing recycled contents, non-toxic chemicals	562	74.93
6.	Products contents under approved chemicals	501	66.80
7.	Products that do not harm or pollute the environment	498	66.40
8.	Products that will not be tested on animals	538	71.73
9.	Products that have eco-friendly packaging	453	60.40

Source: Primary Data

From the data analysis presented above, it has been inferred that 77.73 per cent of the respondents have said that they identified the green products through the nature ingredients used in manufacturing of the products. 74.93 per cent of the respondents have commented that green products contain qualities like recyclable, non-toxic chemicals etc. Whereas, 71.73 per cent of the respondents believe that green products are not tested on animals. A batch of 66.80 per cent of the respondents have opined that green products contain approved chemicals, by which the consumers can recognise a product as green and 66.40 per cent of the respondents believe that green products do not harm or pollute the environment.

Among 750 respondents surveyed, 64.27 per cent of the respondents claim that green products are recyclable, reusable and biodegradable and 61.87 per cent of the respondents have said that these products are naturally grown. On the contrary, 60.40 per cent of the respondents have said that when a product is packed with eco–friendly materials it can be treated as environmentally friendly.

A batch of 56.27 per cent of the respondents claim that green products save energy and these products can be identified through the product quality.

In short, it has been inferred that 77.73 per cent of the respondents have said that they identify the green products through the nature ingredients used in manufacturing the product like cosmetics, home-cleaning products, disinfectants, packing materials etc. For example aloe vera gel turmeric, neem leaf and its barks, mud, clay, wood and wood pulp, jute etc.

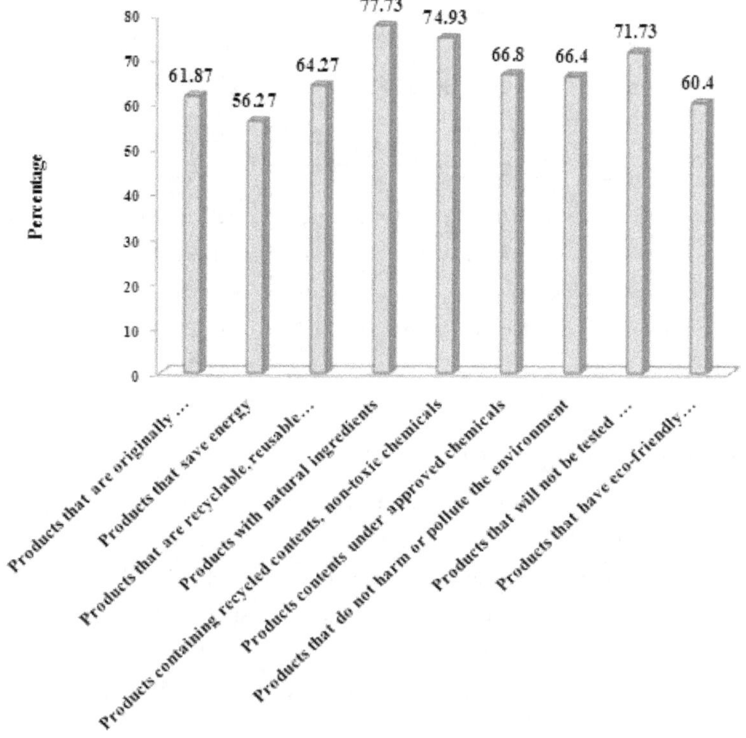

Identification of Green Prodcuts

Exhibit 4.1: Consumers Opinion on Parameters Considered for Identification of Green Products

Consumers' awareness and motivation continue to drive change in the marketplace, notably through the introduction of more green products. Compared to consumers in the developed countries, the Indian consumer has more awareness of global warming issues. In India, successful green marketing has always been about recognizing trends and positioning of products, services and brand in a manner that supports buyers' intentions. Today, "Green" marketing has moved from a trend to a way of doing business and businesses that sell green products should recognise (a) the value of going green and (b) incorporating this message into their marketing programme and communicating the green concept to their consumers. This discussion clearly says that consumers' level of awareness towards green products supports them in recognising a product as eco-friendly or non-eco-friendly. To draw an empirical justification to this concept the following hypothesis is framed and tested.

H2: Consumers' level of awareness towards green products does not support them in recognising a product as eco-friendly or non-eco-friendly.

Table 4.14: Result of Chi-Square Consumers' Level of Awareness Towards Green Products

Chi-Square Value	DF	Table value	Remark
585.647	28	41.337	Rejected

From the above table it has been inferred that the calculated chi-square value is greater than the table value of 41.337 at 5 per cent level of significance. Therefore, the hypothesis framed stands rejected and it is concluded that their consumers' level of awareness towards green products helps in recognising a product as eco-friendly or non-eco-friendly. The study finding is found be on par with the conclusion drawn by Nath et al. (2014). Their study found that green advertising and eco-labelling has a significant positive relation to green purchase intentions.

4.1.3. Consumers' Attitude towards Green Products

Consumers' attitude is interrelated between knowing, feeling and doing. Attitude represents what consumers like and dislike. Attitude of environmental concern are rooted in a person's concept of self and the degree to which an individual perceives him or herself to be an integral part of the natural environment. This section of the study draws a detailed analysis on the consumers' attitude towards green products. The following table 4.15 and 4.16 depict the consumers' attitude towards green products and the nature of attitude exhibited while buying green products.

Table 4.15: Consumers' Level of Attitude towards Green Products

Attitude	Very True	True	True to a Certain Extent	False	Very False	Sum	Mean	Rank
Shopping the environmentally friendly product is one of the best options to maintain the well-being of the planet and inhale fresh and clean air	196 (26.13)	509 (67.87)	45 (6.00)	0 (0.00)	0 (0.00)	3151	4.20	2
Purchasing green products will enable the eradication of corruption from the society	81 (10.80)	400 (53.33)	199 (26.53)	70 (9.33)	0 (0.00)	2742	3.66	5
I want to preserve the earth so I prefer buying green products.	203 (27.07)	381 (50.80)	146 (19.47)	20 (2.67)	0 (0.00)	3017	4.02	3
Eco-friendly and biodegradable products are much appealing and cheaper than the products made from other materials	273 (36.40)	226 (30.13)	242 (32.27)	9 (1.20)	0 (0.00)	3013	4.02	3
Green products are better than non-conventional products	273 (36.40)	371 (49.47)	106 (14.13)	0 (0.00)	0 (0.00)	3167	4.22	1

The above table illustrates the consumers' level of attitude towards green products. Majority of consumers believe that green products are better than non-conventional products, this variable is ranked in first place with the mean score of 4.22 i.e. on average 84.40 per cent of the respondents. 84 per cent (mean score of 4.20) of the respondents have commented that purchasing the environmentally friendly product is one of the best options to maintain the well- being of the planet and to inhale fresh and clean air. It was observed that 80.40 per cent (mean score of 4.02) of the respondents have said that they want to preserve the earth so they prefer buying green products and biodegradable products are much appealing, cheaper than the products made from other materials, so they prefer buying it. On the contrary, 73.20 per cent (mean score of 3.66) of the respondents believe that purchasing green products will support in eradication of corruption from the society.

From the above discussion it has been inferred that 84.40 per cent of the respondents (mean score of 4.22) believe that green products are better than non-conventional product. The study indicates that the consumers are more intended to buy green products that cause very less or no harm to self and to the environment.

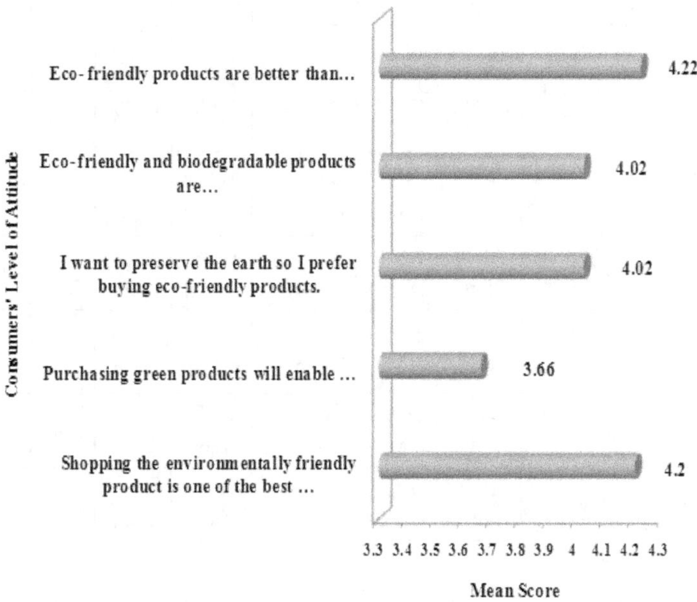

Exhibit 4.2: Consumers' Level of Attitude Towards Green Products

Table 4.16: Nature of Eco-Friendly Attitude Exhibited by the Consumers

Nature	Very True	True	True to a Certain Extent	False	Very False	Sum	Mean	Rank
I would describe myself as environmentally responsible, which is exercised in day- to-day buying behaviors.	128 (17.07)	466 (62.13)	141 (18.80)	15 (2.00)	0 (0.00)	2957	3.94	3
When I purchase products, I try to make efforts to buy products that are low in pollutants.	162 (21.60)	398 (53.07)	190 (25.33)	0 (0.00)	0 (0.00)	2972	3.96	2
I am willing to pay a premium price for an green product	136 (18.13)	397 (52.93)	195 (26.00)	22 (2.93)	0 (0.00)	2897	3.86	5
I pay attention to eco-friendly advertisement	179 (23.87)	380 (50.67)	177 (23.60)	14 (1.87)	0 (0.00)	2974	3.97	1
I pay attention to information Written on product packages	119 (15.87)	416 (55.47)	187 (24.93)	28 (3.73)	0 (0.00)	2876	3.83	6
I pay attention to the nature of ingredients used in the product manufacturing /process.	124 (16.53)	242 (32.27)	335 (44.67)	49 (6.53)	0 (0.00)	2691	3.59	10
I pay attention to product packages design (like paper, tetra packages, recyclable plastics, natural products, glass etc.)	114 (15.20)	256 (34.13)	319 (42.53)	61 (8.13)	0 (0.00)	2673	3.56	11
I pay attention to reputation & genuineness of the ganufacture or processors	139 (18.53)	296 (39.47)	225 (30.00)	90 (12.00)	0 (0.00)	2734	3.65	9
I intend to buy products manufactured locally	168 (22.40)	209 (27.87)	229 (30.53)	123 (16.40)	21 (2.80)	2630	3.51	12
I intend to buy products manufactured by International manufacturers	202 (26.93)	229 (30.53)	228 (30.40)	70 (9.33)	21 (2.80)	2771	3.69	8
I focus on product labelling	265 (35.33)	231 (30.80)	153 (20.40)	60 (8.00)	41 (5.47)	2869	3.83	6
I focus on product quality	316 (42.13)	184 (24.53)	149 (19.87)	60 (8.00)	41 (5.47)	2924	3.90	4

Source: Primary Data

The above table draws discussion on the nature of eco-friendly attitude exhibited by consumers while making purchase decision. It has been observed that majority (79.40 per cent) (mean score of 3.97) of the eco-friendly consumer pay attention to the advertisement claim made about the products and try to frame an attitude towards the product. A batch of 79.20 per cent (mean score of 3.96) of them have said that every time they try to make efforts to buy products that are low in polluting environment. 78.80 per cent (mean score of 3.94) of the respondents are always environmentally responsible i.e., conscious. The study observed that 78 per cent (mean score of 3.90) of the sample population have said that they always focus on the quality of the products.

Where as 77.20 per cent (mean score of 3.86) of the respondents have expressed that they are willing to pay a premium price for an green products.

A batch of 76.60 per cent (mean score of 3.83) of the respondents have said that they develop an attitude on green products by reading the information on product packages and on the product labellers. It was observed that 73.80 per cent (mean score of 3.69) of the respondents have intended to buy green products manufactured by internationally reputed companies.

A batch of 73 per cent (mean score of 3.65) of the respondents believe that reputation and genuineness of the manufacture or processors is important while buying green products. 71.80 per cent (mean score of 3.59) of the respondents have said that they identified the green products through the nature of ingredients used in the product manufacturing /process. Similarly, 71.20 per cent (mean score of 3.56) of the respondents have said they pay attention on product packages design (like: usage of bio-degradable material paper, tetra packages, recyclable plastics, natural products and glass).

Further it has been observed that 70.20 per cent (mean score 3.51) of the respondents have said that they buy products manufactured locally, which in turn ensures authentication of the green products produced in a geographical region.

The study found that majority (79.40per cent) (mean score of 3.97) of the eco-friendly consumers pay attention to the advertisement claim made about the products and try to frame an attitude towards the products. The mass media plays an important role in creating an opinion about green products.

As stated in the TABLE: 4.12, 97.73 per cent of the respondents have sourced information about green products from yoga class, art of living class, seminars, public gathering and from other naturopathy classes etc.

The study has found that mass events and public programmes can contribute decisively to the formation of green products buying behaviour.

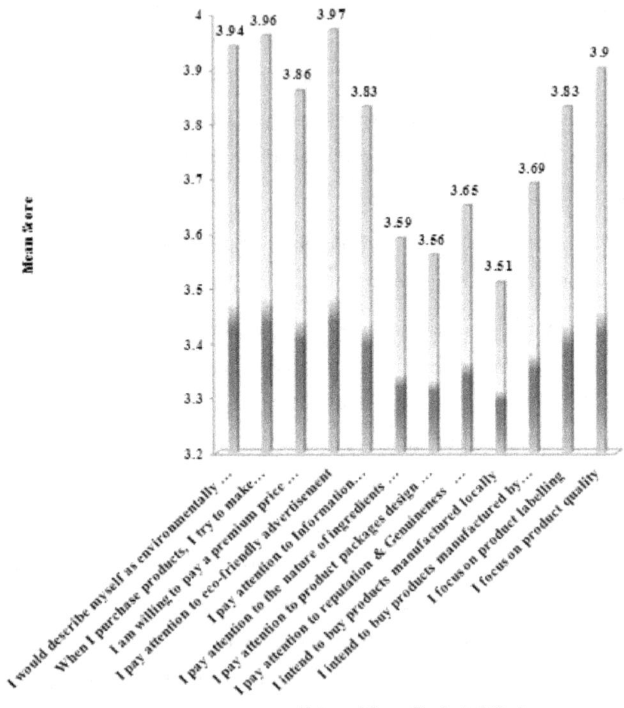

Davidson et al. (1985) found that the consumers' attitude is associated with the knowledge and personal experience they possess. To reassess the feasibility of this statement the following hypothesis is framed and tested the existing association between consumers' awareness and attitude towards green products.

H3: Consumers' level of awareness towards green products greatly influences their level of attitude towards it.

The multiple regression analysis was performed to evaluate whether consumers' level of awareness towards green products influences their level of attitude towards it.

The dependent variable considered was consumers' level of awareness towards green products and the independent variables (Consumers' level of attitude towards green products) are: X_1= Shopping the environmentally friendly product is one of the best options to maintain the well- being of the planet and inhale fresh and clean air, X_2=Purchasing green products will enable the eradication of corruption from the society, X_3= I want to preserve the earth so I prefer buying green products, X_4= Green and biodegradable product are much appealing and cheaper than the product made from other material and X_5= Green products are better than non-conventional products.

Consumers' level of attitude towards green products = f (Shopping the environmentally friendly product is one of the best options to maintain the well- being of the planet and inhale fresh and clean air, Purchasing green products will enable the eradication of corruption from the society, I want to preserve the earth so, I prefer buying green products, green and biodegradable product are much appealing and cheaper than the products made from other materials and green product are better than non-conventional products.)

Measured consumers' level of attitude towards green products was considered as dummy variable and run the following regression model to identify the consumers' level of awareness towards green products. Consumers' level of attitude towards green products = (Y1) = $\beta 0 + \beta 1 X1 + \beta 2 X2 + \beta 3 X3 + \beta 4 X4 + \beta 5 X5 + e$

Where,

Y1   = Consumers' level of attitude towards green products

$\beta 0$ = Intercept

$\beta 1 - \beta 11$= Slopes (estimates of coefficients)

X_1 = Shopping the environmentally friendly products is one of the best options to maintain the wellbeing of the planet and inhale fresh and clean air.

X_2 = Purchasing green products will enable the eradication of corruption from the society

X_3 = I want to preserve the earth, so I prefer buying green products

X_4 = Green and biodegradable products are much appealing and cheaper than the products made from other materials

X_5 = Green products are better than non-conventional products and

e   = Random error, which the researcher assumed as NID for this research.

Table 4.17: Multiple Regression Model Summary Association between Consumers' Level of Awareness Towards Green Products and Their Attitude

R	R^2	Adjusted R^2	SE	F Value	Sig
.248	.061	.055	1.012	9.737	.000

Level of Significance: 5 per cent

$Y = 1.522 - .343\ X_1 + .007\ X_3 + .112\ X_4 + .178\ X_5 - .051$

It has been revealed from the above econometric analysis that F ratio (9.737) is statistically significant at 5 per cent level. This indicates that the entire regression is significant, and it establishes 24.80 per cent of relationship between the variables tested. From the above table it is seen that the coefficient of correlation (R) value .248 which describes a good relationship between variables and the coefficient of determinant (R^2) .061 value establishes a significant association between the 5 variables tested. The hypothesis framed stands accepted and it has been concluded that consumers' level of awareness towards green products is influenced by their level of attitude towards it. The conclusion of the study found relevance with the conclusion drawn by Gan et al. (2008). Their study concluded by stating that green product attributes play a very important role in product development since they affect consumers' product choices and they help marketers to satisfy customers' needs, wants and demands.

The following table shows the value of constant and coefficient value of each attributes to analyse the consumers' attitude towards green products.

Table 4.18: Association Between Consumers' Level of Awareness Towards Green Products and their Attitude

Variables	Unstandardized Coefficients		Standardized Coefficients	t	Sig
	β	Std. Error	Beta		
Constant	1.522	.204	-	7.459	.000
Shopping the environmentally friendly products is one of the best options to maintain the well-being of the planet and inhale fresh and clean air.	.343	.075	.175	4.563	.000
Purchasing green products will enable the eradication of corruption from the society	.007	.051	.006	.144	.886
I want to preserve the earth, so I prefer buying green products.	.112	.051	.081	2.174	.030
Eco-friendly and biodegradable products are much appealing and cheaper than the product made from other materials.	.178	.045	.146	3.932	.000
Green products are better than Non-conventional product.	-.051	.060	-.033	-.841	.401

Level of Significance: 5 per cent

To determine of one or more of the independent variables are significant with the predictors and to analyse whether the consumers' level of awareness towards green products influences their level of attitude towards it with the information provided above the co-efficient table is examined.

Out of five parameters statements considered only three were statistically significant. The standardized co-efficient beta column reveals that consumers' level of attitude towards green products have met beta standard co-efficient 1.522 which is statistically significant at 0.000.

Predicated Value of

Consumers' level of attitude towards green products

= +.1.522 (Constant)

+.343 (Shopping the environmentally friendly products is one of the best options to maintain the well-being of the planet and inhale fresh and clean air.)

+.112 (I want to preserve the earth, so I prefer buying green products.)

+.178 (Eco-friendly and biodegradable products are much appealing and cheaper than the products made from other materials.)

To assess the consumers' level of attitude towards green products multiple regression modeling was performed and to the relative importance of the individual dimension of the generated scale.

Multiple Regression Analysis indicated out of five variables tested three variables: Shopping the environmentally friendly products is one of the best options to maintain the well-being of the planet and inhale fresh and clean air, they also commented that they prefer buying green products as the wish to preserve the earth and eco-friendly and biodegradable products are much appealing and cheaper than the products made from other materials were found to be significant.

4.1.4.   Green Products Buying Behaviour among Consumers

Modern day consumers' consumption decisions of purchase have changed towards products that are greener, more suitable and more environmentally friendly due to the rise in their awareness of current environmental matters.

Green products buying behaviour is influenced by family factors, society factors and government factors and traditional factors like brand names, prices, quality etc. This section of the study draws an elaborate and introspective analysis on the consumers' buying behaviour towards green products in Coimbatore city.

Consumers are becoming more interested in environmentally friendly products this can be best exhibited in the buying behaviour.

The following Tables 4.19 to 4.28 draw a discussion on this concept.

Table 4.19: Consumers' Buying Behaviour Towards Green Products

Sl. No	Buying Behaviour	No. of Respondents	Percentage
1.	Always	199	26.53
2.	Often	245	32.67
3.	Occasionally	306	40.80
	Total	750	100

Source: Primary Data

From the above data table it has been inferred that 40.80 per cent of the respondents always prefer buying green products. 32.67 per cent of the respondents have said that they often buy green products. On the contrary 26.53 per cent f the respondents have said that they occasionally buy green products.

Hence it has been concluded that majority of i.e. 40.80 per cent of the respondents have said that they always prefer buying green products. Due to several reasons like lack of awareness about the features of green products, poor product promotions, poor product availability or usage among modern households, green products acceptance is comparatively less among the sample population surveyed in Coimbatore city.

Table 4.20: Consumers' Opinion on Influences of Referral Group on their Buying Behaviour

Sl. No	Influence	No. of Respondents	Percentage
1.	Self –References	265	35.33
2.	Friends & Colleagues	273	36.40
3.	Family Members & Relatives	170	22.67
4.	Salespersons	42	5.60
	Total	750	100

Source: Primary Data

From the above data table it has been referred that 36.40 per cent of the respondents have said that friends and colleagues mostly influence their perception towards green products and their values. 35.33 per cent of the respondents have said that they themselves learned about the benefits of green products.

On the contrary, 22.67 per cent of the respondents have taken the advice of family members and relatives and 5.60 per cent of the respondents have said that they gathered information about green products from the salespersons.

Hence it has been concluded that 36.40 per cent of the respondents have said that friends and colleagues mostly influence consumers' perception towards green products and its values. It is understood that pattern of peer group members greatly influence green products buying practices of the respondents.

Table 4.21: Consumers' Opinion on Longevity of Buying Green Products

Sl. No	Long Period	No. of Respondents	Percentage
1.	1-3 years	442	58.93
2.	3-5 years	166	22.13
3.	6-8 years	47	6.27
4.	For many years	95	12.67
	Total	750	100

From the above data table it has been inferred that 58.93 per cent of the respondents have been consuming green products for the past 1-3 years. 22.13 per cent of the respondents have used green products for 3-5 years and 12.67 per cent of the respondents have been using green products for many years. The remaining 6.27 per cent of the respondents have said that they have been consuming green products for the past 6-8 years.

From the above discussion it has been inferred that 58.93 per cent of the respondents have been consuming green products for the past 1-3 years. Consumers now have to worry about the future of the world and they have started to give priority to environmentally friendly products. This fear of the consumers has been best emphasized on longevity of purchasing green products.

Table 4.22: Nature of Green Products Bought by the Consumers

Sl. No	Nature	No. of Respondents N=5658	Proportionate Percentage
1.	Organic Cereals & Pulses	447	59.60
2.	Organic Masala Products	474	63.20
3.	Organic Processed Food Products	444	59.20
4.	Organic Home Furniture	325	43.33
5.	Solar or Wind Power	397	52.93
6.	Electrical Goods	493	65.73
7.	Electronic Goods	531	70.80
8.	Cooking Vessels	541	72.13
9.	Herbal Medicines and Cosmetics	546	72.80
10.	Wood - Based Products	568	75.73
11.	Hair Oils and Cooking Oils	436	58.13
12.	Jute and Coir product	456	60.80

The data presented in the above table clearly indicates that 75.73 per cent of the respondents are keen to buy wood-based products. 72.80 per cent of the respondents usually buy herbal medicines and cosmetics product, 72.13 per cent of the respondents buy cooking vessels like mud pots, wooden spatulas and 70.80 per cent of the respondents are interested in buying electronic goods. Further, it has been observed that 65.73 per cent of the respondents buy electrical goods. Similarly, 63.20 per cent of the respondents prefer buying organic masala products, 60.80 per cent of the respondents like to shop for jute and coir products and 59.60 per cent of the household consumers prefer to shop for organic cereals and pulses. The study found that 59.20 per cent of the respondents usually buy organic processed food products and 58.13 per cent of the respondents are interested in buying hair oils and cooking oils. Correspondingly 52.93 per cent of the respondents prefer to buy solar or wind power products and 43.33 per cent of the respondents buy wooden or eco-friendly home furniture items.

From the above discussion it has been inferred that majority (75.73 per cent) of the respondents are found to buy wooden products.

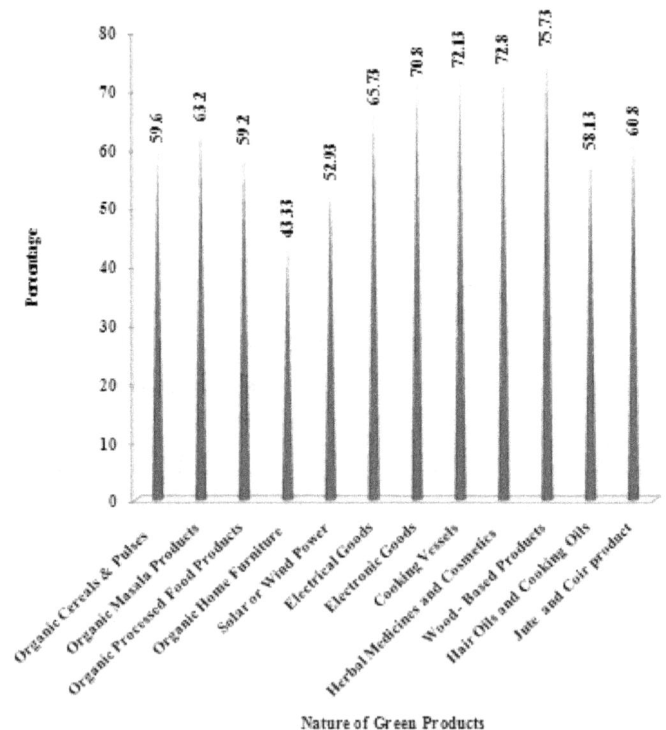

Exhibit 4.4: Nature of Green Products Bought by the Consumers

Table 4.23: Consumers' Opinion on Factors that Influence them Towards Green Products

Factors	Sum	Mean	Rank
Made out of natural products	3879	5.17	12
Eco-friendly labels and marks	4133	5.51	11
Price	3863	5.15	13
Product quality	4508	6.01	10
Offers & discounts	5192	6.92	8
Product promotion	5678	7.57	5
Innovative design of the product	5980	7.97	4
Product usefulness	4975	6.63	9
Bio-degradable	5548	7.40	7
Recycling/Reuse features	6030	8.04	3
Environmental knowledge& Concern/Care	5563	7.42	6
Ethnic feature of the product	6035	8.05	2
Long usage in the family	6370	8.49	1

Source: Primary Data

The above table discusses the factors that influence consumers to purchase green products. Majority of consumers have said that long usage of organic products in the family greatly influenced their adoption towards modern day innovative green products and this variable is ranked in first place with the mean score of 8.49. Ethnic feature of the product, recycling/reuse features, innovative design of the product, product promotion are factors that influence most of the consumers surveyed. These factors are ranked in second, third, fourth and fifth place with the mean score of 8.05, 8.04, 7.97 and 7.57 respectively. Similarly, consumers' environmental knowledge and concern or care, bio-degradable, offers and discounts available while shopping green products, product usefulness and product quality are factors that moderately influence consumers to buy green products. These factors are ranked in sixth, seventh, eighth, ninth and tenth place with the mean score of 7.42, 7.40, 6.92, 6.63 and 6.01 respectively. Likewise eco-friendly labels and marks, made out of natural products (ecological) and price factors had a low level of influence on the consumers of green products. These factors are ranked in eleventh, twelfth and thirteenth place with the mean score of 5.51, 5.17 and 5.15 separately.

From the data discussion it has been inferred that 65.31per cent (8.49 Mean Score) of the respondents have said that long usage of organic products in the family greatly influenced their adoption towards green products. The study clearly indicates that consuming green products is part of Indian tradition and also part of our societal lifestyle. This is because the people in India have a general inclination towards need-based consumption and an ingrained sense of responsibility toward environments.

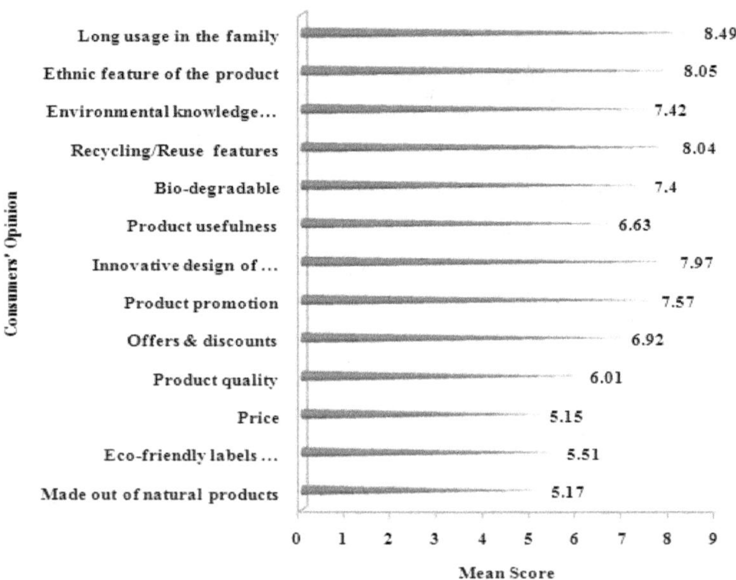

Exhibit 4.5: Consumers' Opinion on Factors that Influence Them Towards Green Products

In marketing theories it has been said that the purchase decisions of green consumers are influenced by broadly two factors. One set of factors is intrinsic to the consumers such as realization of their environmental responsibilities, quest for gaining knowledge, self-interest and willingness to act for resource conservation and reduced impact on the environment. And, the others set of factors extrinsic to the consumers which are related to, for example, social image of consumers and product characteristics (such as product quality, safety, performance, price, promotion and impact on human health). It is believed that consumers buying behaviour is influenced by these two intrinsic and extrinsic factors. The following hypothesis is framed based on the understanding drawn from above discussion.

H4: The factors that influence consumers for buying green products do not differ from one individual to another.

Table 4.24: Result of Kendall's Co-Efficient of Concordance Consumers' Opinion on Factors that Influence them Towards Green Products

W	S	Level of Significance	Chi-Square Value	Table Value
.089	750	5 per cent	805.083	21.026

Level of significance: 5 per cent

From the above table it has been inferred that the calculated chi-square value is greater than the table values 21.026 at 5 per cent level of significance. Therefore, the hypothesis framed stands rejected and it is concluded that the factors that influence consumers for buying green products differ from one individual to another. The conclusion drawn in this section has found its relevance with the conclusion made by Kumar and Ghodeswar (2015). The authors claimed in their study that green products experience, environmental friendliness of companies and social appeal are identified as important factors affecting green products purchase decisions among various categories of consumers. The study conducted by Ramayah et al. (2010) and Moisander's (2007) study focused to assess the factors that motivate and influence green purchase behaviour of consumers. The study found that green purchase behaviour represents a complex form of ethical decision-making behaviour and is considered a type of socially responsible behaviour. As a socially responsible consumer, the green consumer "takes into account the public consequences of his or her private consumption and attempts to use his or her purchasing power to bring about social change".

Explorative factor analysis technique has been applied to find the underlying dimension (factors) that exists in the thirteen variables relating to the factor that influences consumer to buy green products.

Table 4.25: KMO and Bartlett's Testfactors that Influence the Consumers to Buy Green Products

Kaiser-Meyer-Olkin Measure of Sampling Adequacy	.748
Bartlett's Test of Sphericity Approx. Chi-Square	4983.629
DF	78
Sig	.000

Level of Significance: 5 per cent

In the present study, Kaiser-Meyer-Oklin (KMO) Measure of Sampling Adequacy (MSA) and Bartlett's test of Sphericity were applied to verify the adequacy or appropriateness of data for factor analysis.

In this study, the value of KMO for overall matrix was found to be excellent (0.748) and Bartlett's test of Sphericity was highly significant (p<0.05).

Bartlett's Sphericity test was effective, as the chi-square value draws significance at five per cent level. The results thus indicated that the sample taken was appropriate to proceed with factor analysis procedure. Besides Bartlett's Test of Sphericity and KMO Measure of sampling Adequacy, Communality values of all variables were also observed.

Table 4.26: Cumulative Factors that Influence the Consumers to Buy Green Products

Factors	Initial	Extraction
Made out of natural products (Ecological)	1.000	.808
Eco-friendly labels & Marks	1.000	.809
Price	1.000	.751
Product quality	1.000	.810
Offers & Discounts	1.000	.722
Product promotion	1.000	.783
Innovative design of the product	1.000	.851
Product usefulness	1.000	.590
Bio-Degradable	1.000	.831
Recycling/Reuse features	1.000	.684
Environmental knowledge and Concern/Care	1.000	.652
Ethnic feature of the product	1.000	.799
Long usage in the family	1.000	.655

In order to provide a more parsimonious interpretation of the results, 13-item scale was then factor analyzed using the Principal Component method with Varimax rotation. Factor analysis attempts to identify the underlying variables, or factors, that explain the pattern of correlations within a set of observed variables. Factor analysis is often used in data reduction to identify a small number of factors that explain most of the variance observed in a much larger number of manifest variables. In the current study rotation factor analysis is performed to measure the factors that influence consumers to buy green products. The significance of relationship between the variables is depicted in the following table

Table 4.27: Rotated Component Matrix Factors that Nfluence the Consumers to Buy Green Products

Factors	Factors				
	F_1	F_2	F_3	F_4	F_5
X_1- Made out of natural products (Ecological)	-	.777	-	-	-
X_2- Eco-friendly labels & Marks	-	.759	-	-	-
X_3- Price	.657	-			
X_4- Product quality	-	-		.837	-
X_5- Offers & Discounts	-	-	.759	-	-
X_6- Product promotion	-	-	.850	-	-
X_7- Innovative design of the product	-	-	-	.766	-
X_8- Product usefulness	-	.588	-	-	-
X_9- Bio-Degradable	-		-	-	.847
X_{10} Recycling/Reuse features	-	.696	-	-	-
X_{11}- Environmental knowledge and Concern/Care	.758	-	-	-	-
X_{12}- Ethnic feature of the product	.859	-	-	-	-
X_{13}- Long usage in the family	.718	-	-	-	-
Eigen value	2.693	2.381	1.806	1.555	1.312
% of Variance	20.714	18.312	13.891	11.960	10.093
Cumulative	20.714	39.026	52.918	64.878	74.971

Level of Significance: 5 per cent

Through an analysis of items in each factor, new dimensions were defined (Table 4.27), excluding items with a value lower than 0.5. Five factors extracted together account for 74.971 per cent of the total variance (information contained in the original 13 variables). This is good, because the researcher is able to economize on the number of variables (from 13 researcher have reduced them to five underlying factors), while the data lost only about 25.029 per cent of the information content (74.971 per cent is retained by the five factors extracted out of the 13 original variables). Since the idea of factor analysis is to identify the factors that meaningfully summarize the sets of closely related variables, the rotation phase of the factor analysis attempts to transfer initial matrix into one that is easier to interpret. Varimax rotation method is used to extract meaningful factors.

Five factors were identified as being maximum percentage variance accounted. The variable X3, X11, X12 and X13 is grouped as factor I and it accounts for 20.714 per cent of the total variance. The variables X1, X2, X8, and X10 constitute the factor II and it accounts for 18.312 per cent of the total variance. The variable X5 and X6 constitute the factor III and it accounts for 13.891 per cent of the total variance. The variable X4 and X7 constitute the factor IV and it accounts for 11.960 per cent of the total variance. The variable X9 constitute the factor V and it accounts for 10.093 per cent of the total variance.

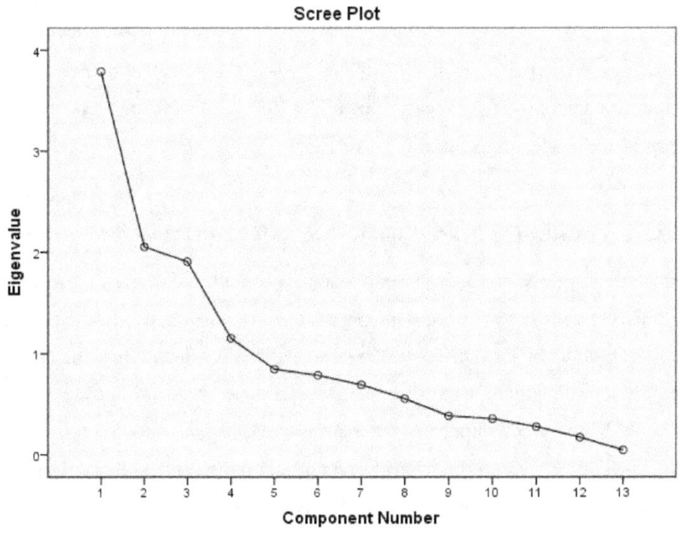

Exhibit 4.6: Scree Plot Factors that Influence the Consumers

TO BUY GREEN PRODUCTS: A Scree plot is a graph that plots the total variance associated with each factor. It is a visual display of how many factors there are in the data. The Scree plot graphs the Eigenvalue against the factor number. It has been observed that although there are 13 principal components only 4 factors have Eigenvalues over one. So it can expect three principal components in the data. The curve indicates the inflexion on the curve.

Table 4.28: Summary of Rotation Factor Analysis & Cronbach's Alpha Factors that Influence the Consumers to Buy Green Products

Factors	Factor Interpretation	Variables included in the factors	Cronbach's Alpha
F_1	Highly Satisfied	Price, Environmental knowledge and Concern/care, Ethnic feature of the product, Long Usage in the family.	.949
F_2	Satisfied	Made out of natural products (Ecological), eco-friendly labels & marks, product usefulness, recycling/reuse features.	.932
F_3	Moderately Satisfied	Offers & discounts, product promotion.	.928
F_4	Dissatisfied	Product quality, innovative design of the product.	.917
F_5	Highly Dissatisfied	Bio-degradable.	.908

Source: Computed From Primary Data

The internal consistency of each factor was estimated individually using the alpha coefficient of Cronbach's (α).

Factor analysis was applied to establish and reveal the correlation between factors that influenced the consumers to buy green products. The Cronbach's reliability values of (.949, .932, .928, .917, and .908) indicate significant correlation between the variables tested and a good internal consistency.

4.1.5. *Consumers Level of Perception and Satisfaction towards Green Products*

Consumers' perceptions towards green products generally influence their decision-making process and buying behaviour. Consumers' perceptions towards green products represent the formation of an individual state of mental awareness that is affected by internal and external environmental stimuli such as economic, social and cultural influences. Moreover, environmentally friendly consumers buy the products that best satisfy their expectations of eco-friendly concepts. Based on this conceptual understanding this section of the study draws a detailed analysis on the consumers' perception towards green products.

The measure of consumers' perception towards green products is briefly discussed in the Tables 4.29 to 4.35.

Table 4.29: Consumers' Level of Perception towards Green Products

Perception	Very True	True	True to a Certain Extent	False	Very False	Sum	Mean	Rank
Green products help in protecting the environment	210 (28.00)	476 (63.47)	64 (8.53)	0 (0.00)	0 (0.00)	3146	4.19	3
Green products are healthier	285 (38.00)	446 (59.47)	19 (2.53)	0 (0.00)	0 (0.00)	3266	4.35	1
Green products are Safer	253 (33.73)	417 (55.60)	80 (10.67)	0 (0.00)	0 (0.00)	3173	4.23	2
Green products have less toxic materials	171 (22.80)	426 (56.80)	153 (20.40)	0 (0.00)	0 (0.00)	3018	4.02	7
Green products are easily recyclable or degradable	289 (38.53)	337 (44.93)	103 (13.73)	21 (2.80)	0 (0.00)	3144	4.19	3
Green Products are easily available (Indigenously)	148 (19.73)	372 (49.60)	218 (29.07)	12 (1.60)	0 (0.00)	2906	3.87	8
Green products have a good quality and performance	172 (22.93)	296 (39.47)	269 (35.87)	13 (1.73)	0 (0.00)	2877	3.84	9
Green products have been traditionally used by our ancestors	314 (41.87)	164 (21.87)	252 (33.60)	20 (2.67)	0 (0.00)	3022	4.03	6
There has been proven record for the usage of environmental products and their benefits.	321 (42.80)	167 (22.27)	243 (32.40)	19 (2.53)	0 (0.00)	3040	4.05	5

Source: Primary Data

The above table illustrates the consumers' level of perception towards of green products. Majority of the respondents believe that green products are healthier and safer; these variables are ranked in first and second places with the mean score of 4.35 and 4.23 respectively. Similarly it has been inferred that the sample populations are helping to protect the environment through buying green products, so they prefer buying easily recyclable or degradable green products. This perception is ranked in third place with the mean score of 4.19. Further, it has been observed that the respondents have developed trust on the proven record for the usage of environmental products & their benefits and green products have been traditionally used by our ancestors. These variables are placed in the fifth and sixth places with mean score of 4.05 and 4.03 respectively. The study found that the respondents have exhibited low levels of perception to the belief that green products have lesser amount of toxic materials, these products are easily available in the market and to the belief that green products have a good quality and performance. These variables are ranked in seventh, eighth and ninth places with mean score of 4.02, 3.87 and 3.84 respectively.

The study findings indicated that majority (mean score of 4.35) of respondents believe that green products are healthier and safer.

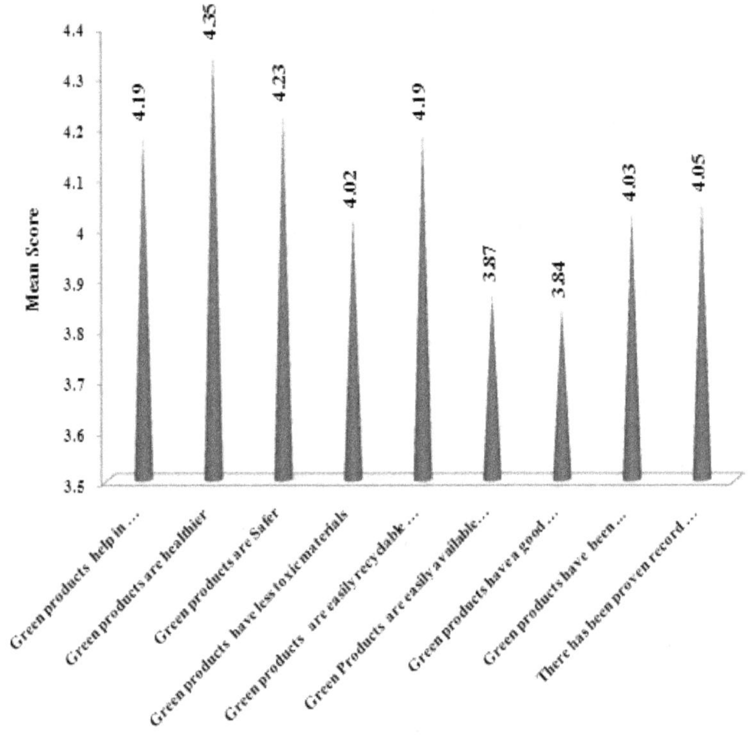

Exhibit 4.7: Consumers' Level of Perception Towards Green Products

The green movement has been expanding rapidly in the world. With regard to this, the consumers are taking responsibility and doing the right things. Consumers' awareness and attitude continue to drive change in the marketplace, notably through the introduction of more green products. Based on this concept it is believed that consumers' level of attitude towards green products may influence their level of perceptions towards it. To draw a feasibility test to the above-mentioned statement the following hypothesis is framed and tested with multiple regression analysis.

H5: Consumers' level of attitude towards green products greatly influences their level of perceptions towards it.

The multiple regression analysis was performed to evaluate whether the consumers' level of attitude towards green products is influenced by their perceptions towards it.

The dependent variable considered was consumers' level of attitude towards green products and the independent variables (Consumers' level of perception towards green products) are: X_1= Green products help in protecting the environment, X_2= Green products are healthier, X_3= Green products are safer, X_4= Green products have less toxic materials, X_5= Green products are easily recyclable or degradable, X_6= Green product are easily available ,X_7= Green products have a good quality& performance, X_8 = Green products have been traditionally used by our ancestors and X_9= There has been proven record for the usage of environmental products & their benefits.

Consumers' level of perception towards green products = f (Green products help in protecting the environment, Green products are healthier, Green products are safer, Green products have less toxic materials, Green products are easily recyclable or degradable, Green product are easily available, Green products have a good quality& performance, Green products have been traditionally used by our ancestors and There has been proven record for the usage of environmental products & their benefits)

Measured consumers' level of perception towards green products was considered as dummy variable and run the following regression model to identify the Consumers' level of attitude towards green a product is influences by their level of perceptions towards it.

Consumers' level of perception towards green products (Y1) = $\beta0 + \beta1X1 + \beta2X2 + \beta3X3 + \beta4X4 + \beta5X5 + \beta6X6 + \beta7X7 + \beta8X8 + \beta9X9 + e$

Where,

Y1= Consumers' level of perception towards green products

$\beta0$ = Intercept

$\beta1 - \beta11$= Slopes (estimates of coefficients

X_1= Green products help in protecting the environment

X_2= Green products are healthier

X_3= Green products are Safer

X_4= Green products have less toxic materials

X_5= Green products are easily recyclable or degradable

X_6= Green products are easily available

X_7= Green products have a good quality& performance,

X_8= Green products have been traditionally used by our ancestors

X_9= There has been proven record for the usage of environmental products & its benefits and

e = Random error, which the researcher assumed as NID for this research.

Table 4.30: Multiple Regression Model Summary Association between Consumers' Level of Attitude and Perception Towards Green Products

R	R²	Adjusted R²	SE	F Value	Sig
.542	.294	.285	.32023	16.919	.000

Level of Significance: 5 per cent

$$Y=1.305+.203X_1+.235X_2+.024X_3-.016X_4-.019X_5+.121X_6-.083X_7-.108X_8+.038\ X_9$$

It has been revealed from the above econometric analysis that F ratio (16.919) is statistically significant at 5 per cent level. This indicates that the entire regression is significant, and it establishes 54.20 per cent of relationship between the variables tested. From the above table it is seen that the coefficient of correlation (R) value .542 describes a good relationship between variables and the coefficient of determinant (R^2) .294 value establishes significant association between the 9 variables tested. The hypothesis framed stands accepted and it has been concluded that consumers' level of attitude towards green products influences their level of perceptions towards it. The study found its relevance with the conclusion made by Terenggana et al. (2013).

The study found that the variable consumer trust is an important factor and a central point which variables significantly influence attitudes, risk perception, perceived quality and consumer purchase intent. Similarly, Cervellon et al. (2010) and Yiridoe et al. (2005) study demonstrated that the demand of green products is increasing day by day all over the world and as such there is concern for understanding how green is a green product. One of the most important restrains to the development of green products is the lack of consumer trust and the lack of information. This shows us that consumers' attitude and perception play an important role in promoting the green product.

The following table shows the value of constant and coefficient value of each attributes to analyse the Consumers' level of attitude towards green products.

Table 4.31: Association between Consumers' Level of Attitude and Perception towards Green Products

Variables	Unstandardized Coefficients		Standardized Coefficients	t	Sig.
	B	Std. Error	Beta		
Constant	1.305	.065	-	20.227	.000
Green products help in protecting the environment	.203	.024	.307	8.451	.000
Green products are healthier	.235	.028	.329	8.529	.000
Green products are Safer	.024	.023	.040	1.055	.292
Green products have less toxic materials	-.016	.021	-.027	-.764	.445
Green products are easily recyclable or degradable	-.019	.018	-.038	-1.040	.299
Green products are easily available	.121	.020	.235	6.147	.000
Green products have a good quality& performance	-.083	.017	-.175	-5.005	.000
Green products have been traditionally used by our ancestors	-.108	.049	-.265	-2.225	.026
There has been proven record for the usage of environmental products & their benefits	.038	.049	.093	.789	.430

Level of Significance: 5 per cent

To determine of one or more of the independent variables are significant with the predictors and to analyse whether consumers' level of attitude towards green products is influenced by their perceptions towards it with the information provided above the co-efficient table is examined. Out of nine parameters statements considered only five were statistically significant. The standardized co-efficient beta column reveals that consumers' level of perception towards green products have met beta standard co-efficient of ±1.305 which is statistically significant at 0.000.

Predicated Value of

Consumers' level of perception towards green products =

+.1305 (Constant)

+.203 (Green products help in protecting the environment)

+.235 (Green products are healthier)

+.121 (Green products are easily available)

±.083 (Green products have a good quality & performance)

+.108 (Green products have been traditionally used by our ancestors)

To assess whether the consumers' level of perceptions towards green products the multiple regression modeling was performed and to the relative importance of the individual dimension of the generated scale, Multiple Regression Analysis indicated that out of nine variables tested five variables: Green products help in protecting the environment, Green products are healthier, Green products are easily available, Green products have a good quality & performance and Green products have been traditionally used by our ancestors these variables were found to be statistically significant.

Explorative Factor analysis technique has been applied to find the underlying dimension (factors) that exists among 9 variables relating to the consumers' level of perception towards green products.

Table 4.32: KMO and Bartlett's Test Consumers' Level of Perception towards Green Products

Kaiser-Meyer-Olkin Measure of Sampling Adequacy	.830
Bartlett's Test of Sphericity Approx. Chi-Square	2994.260
DF	36
Sig	.000

Level of Significance: 5 per cent

In the present study, Kaiser-Meyer-Oklin (KMO) Measure of Sampling Adequacy (MSA) and Bartlett's test of Sphericity were applied to verify the adequacy or appropriateness of data for factor analysis. In this study, the value of KMO for overall matrix was found to be excellent (.830) and Bartlett's test of Sphericity was highly significant (p<0.05). Bartlett's Sphericity test was effective, as the chi-square value draws significance at five per cent level. The results thus indicated that the sample taken was appropriate to proceed with a factor analysis procedure. Besides Bartlett's Test of Sphericity and KMO Measure of sampling Adequacy, Communality values of all variables were also observed.

Table 4.33: Cumulative Consumers' Level of Perception towards Green Products

Factors	Initial	Extraction
Green products help in protecting the environment	1.000	.896
Green products are healthier	1.000	.856
Green products are Safer	1.000	.611
Green products have less toxic materials	1.000	.913
Green products are easily recyclable or degradable	1.000	.533
Green products are easily available (Indigenously)	1.000	.799
Green products have a good quality& performance	1.000	.912
Green products have been traditionally used by our ancestors	1.000	.981
There has been proven record for the usage of environmental products & their benefits	1.000	.977

Level of Significance: 5 per cent

In order to provide a more parsimonious interpretation of the results, 9-item scale was then factor analyzed using the Principal Component method with Varimax rotation. Factor analysis attempts to identify the underlying variables, or factors, that explain the pattern of correlations within a set of observed variables. Factor analysis is often used in data reduction to identify a small number of factors that explain most of the variance observed in a much larger number of manifest variables. In the current study rotation factor analysis is performed to measure the consumer level of perception towards green products. The significance of relationship between the variables is depicted in the following table.

Table 4.34: Rotated Component Matrix Consumers' Level of Perception towards Green Products

Factors	Factors				
	F_1	F_2	F_3	F_4	F_5
X_1- Green products help in protecting the environment	-	-	-	-	.909
X_2- Green products are healthier	-	.806	-	-	-
X_3- Green products are Safer	-	.750	-	-	-
X_4- Green products have less toxic materials,	-	-	-	.934	-
X_5- Green products are easily recyclable or degradable	-	.620	-	-	-
X_6- Green products are easily available (Indigenously)	-	-	.592	-	-
X_7- Green products have a good quality& performance	-	-	.924	-	-
X_8- Green products have been traditionally used by our ancestors	.980	-	-	-	-
X_9-There has been proven record for the usage of environmental products & their benefits.	.979	-	-	-	-
Eigen value	1.991	1.879	1.252	1.181	1.174
% of Variance	22.126	20.880	13.914	13.121	13.040
Cumulative%	22.126	43.006	56.921	70.041	83.081

Level of Significance: 5 per cent

Through an analysis of items in each factor, new dimensions were defined (Table 4.34), excluding items with a value lower than 0.5. Five factors extracted together account for 83.081 per cent of the total variance (information contained in the original 9 variables). This is pretty good, because the researcher is able to economize on the number of variables (from 9, the researcher has reduced them to five underlying factors), while the data lost only about 16.919 per cent of the information content (83.081 per cent is retained by the five factors extracted out of the 9 original variables). Since the idea of factor analysis is to identify the factors that meaningfully summarize the sets of closely related variables, the rotation phase of the factor analysis attempts to transfer initial matrix into one that is easier to interpret. Varimax rotation method is used to extract meaningful factors.

Five factors were identified as being maximum percentage variance accounted. The variables X_8 and X_9 are grouped as factor I and it accounts for 22.126 per cent of the total variance. The variables X_2, X_3 and X_5 constitute the factor II and it accounts for 20.880 per cent of the total variance.

The variables X_6 and X_7 are grouped as factor III and it accounts for 13.914 per cent of the total variance. The variable X_4 is grouped as factor IV and it accounts for 13.121 per cent of the total variance. The variable X1 constitutes the factor V and it accounts for 13.040 per cent of the total variance.

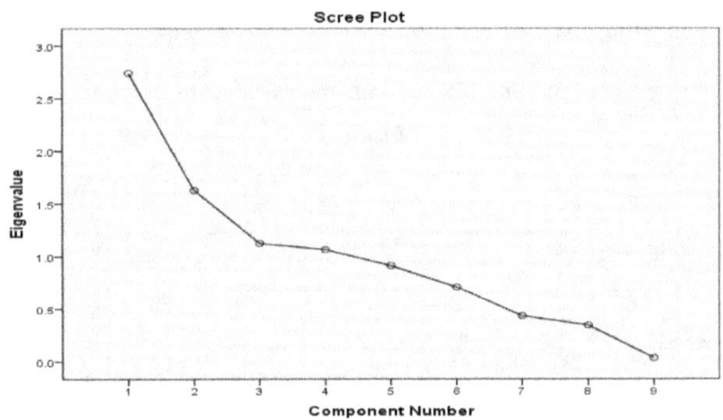

Exhibit 4.8: Scree Plotconsumers' Level Of Perception towards Green Products

A Scree plot is a graph that plots the total variance associated with each factor. It is a visual display of how many factors there are in the data. The Scree plot graphs the Eigenvalue against the factor number. It has been observed that although there are 9 principal components only 3 factors have Eigenvalues over one. So it can expect three principal components in the data. The curve indicates the inflexion on the curve.

Table 4.35: Summary of Rotation Factor Analysis & Cronbach's Alpha Consumers' Level of Perception towards Green Products

Factors	Variables Included in the Factors	Cronbach's Alpha
F_1	Green products have been traditionally used by our ancestors, There has been proven record for the usage of environmental products & their benefits.	.791
F_2	Green products are healthier, Green products are Safer, and green products are easily recyclable or degradable.	.735
F_3	Green products are easily available (Indigenously), Green products have a good quality& performance	.639
F_4	Green products have less toxic materials,	.626
F_5	Green products help in protecting the environment	.606

The internal consistency of each factor was estimated individually using the alpha coefficient of Cronbach's (α). Factor analysis was applied to establish and reveal the correlation between consumers' levels of perception towards green products. The Cronbach's reliability values of

(.791, .735, .639, .626 and .606) indicate significant correlation between the variables tested and a good internal consistency.

The satisfaction of the consumers of green products is of paramount importance because it is more related to their trust towards the products, their loyalty and future buying practices is based on their satisfaction level. With realisation to these facts the analyses are performed in the following tables: from 4.36 to 4.42.

Table 4.36: Consumers' Level of Satisfaction towards Green Products

Satisfaction	Highly Satisfied	Satisfied	Partially Satisfied	Dissatisfied	Highly Dissatisfied	Sum	Mean	Rank
Availability of green products in the market	204 (27.20)	413 (55.07)	133 (17.73)	0 (0.00)	0 (0.00)	3071	4.09	1
Genuineness of the products (Reliability)	135 (18.00)	435 (58.00)	180 (24.00)	0 (0.00)	0 (0.00)	2955	3.94	5
Easy accessibility to green products	118 (15.73)	442 (58.93)	167 (22.27)	23 (3.07)	0 (0.00)	2905	3.87	8
Creative, innovative and modernisation features incorporated in the products	54 (7.20)	492 (65.60)	187 (24.93)	17 (2.27)	0 (0.00)	2833	3.78	10
Price of the products	225 (30.00)	337 (44.93)	154 (20.53)	34 (4.53)	0 (0.00)	3003	4.00	3
Quality of the products	198 (26.40)	325 (43.33)	199 (26.53)	28 (3.73)	0 (0.00)	2943	3.92	6
Promotion of the products	165 (22.00)	319 (42.53)	219 (29.20)	47 (6.27)	0 (0.00)	2852	3.80	9
Offers & Discounts	165 (22.00)	376 (50.13)	179 (23.87)	30 (4.00)	0 (0.00)	2926	3.90	7
Product Varieties Available	148 (19.73)	302 (40.27)	251 (33.47)	49 (6.53)	0 (0.00)	2799	3.73	11
Durability of the product (long-lasting)	226 (30.13)	365 (48.67)	132 (17.60)	27 (3.60)	0 (0.00)	3040	4.05	2
Insurances for eco-friendly features Like labelling	240 (32.00)	344 (45.87)	93 (12.40)	73 (9.73)	0 (0.00)	3001	4.00	3

The above table discusses consumers' level of satisfaction towards green products. On average 4.09 (81.80 per cent) consumers have exhibited high degree of satisfaction towards the green products available in the market. This variable is ranked in first place. On an average 4.05, the respondents have said that they are satisfied with the product durability. It has been inferred that the respondents are satisfied with the green features like labelling and price of the products. These factors are ranked in third rank with an average score of 4.00. Consumers have expressed moderate level of satisfaction towards reputation and genuineness of the products, quality of the products, and offers and discounts. These variables are ranked in fifth, sixth and seventh place with the mean score of 3.94, 3.92 and 3.90 respectively. A batch of consumers have said that they have derived low level of satisfaction with marketing practices of green products like easy accessibility to green products, promotion of the products and creative, innovative and modernisation features incorporated in the product. These factors are ranked in eighth, ninth, and tenth ranks with an average score of 3.87, 3.80 and 3.78

respectively. Further it has been observed that the consumers have exhibited very low level of satisfaction for the green product varieties available in the market; it is ranked in eleventh place with the mean score of 3.73. Thus it has been clearly concluded that majority (81.80 per cent) of the consumers (mean of 4.09 on the Likert's five-point scale) have exhibited high degree of satisfaction towards the green products available in the market.

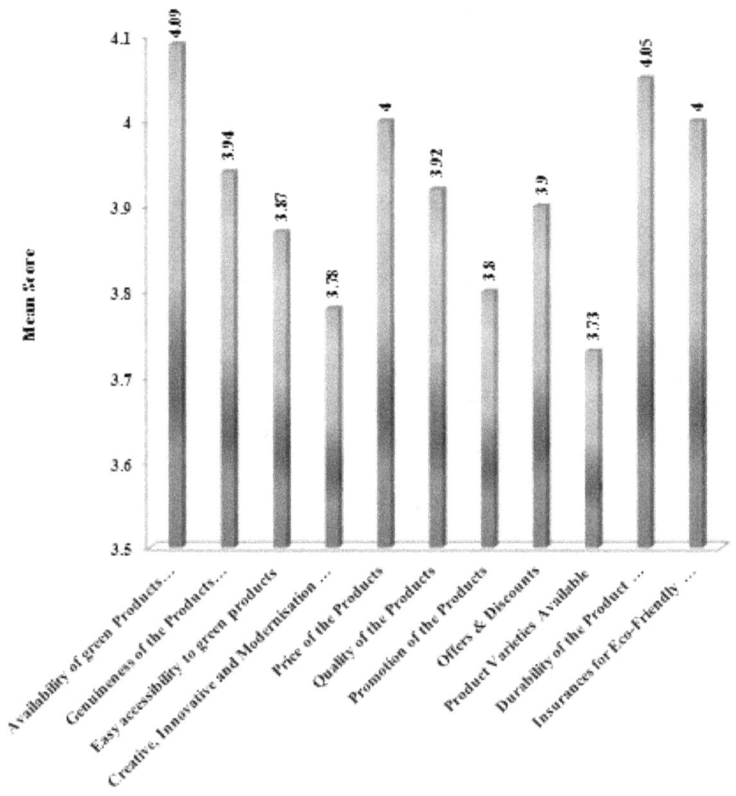

Exhibit 4.9: Consumers' Level of Satisfaction towards Green Products

Success of producing green products will depend on whether consumers will accept the products or not. Consumers' perception towards products depicts their overall judgment about a product and its performances i.e., its superiority or excellence. Thus, it can be rightly claimed that consumers' perception towards the green products can influence their level of satisfaction towards its. Drawing rational motivation from this concept the following hypothesis is framed and tested.

H6: There exists a close association between consumers' level of perception towards green products and level of satisfaction towards it.

The multiple regression analysis was performed to evaluate the existing association between consumers' level of perception towards green products and level of satisfaction towards it.

The dependent variable considered was consumers' level of perception towards green products and the independent variable: X_1 =Availability of green Products in the Market, X_2= Genuineness of the Product (Reliability), X_3= Easy accessibility to green products, X_4= Creative, Innovative and Modernisation Features Incorporated in the Products, X_5= Price of the products X_6= Quality of the Products, X_7= Promotion of the Products, X_8= Offers & Discounts, X_9= Product Varieties Available, X_{10}= Durability of the Product (long-lasting and X_{11}= Insurances for Eco-friendly Features like Labelling.

Consumers' level of satisfaction towards green products = f (Availability of green Products in the Market, Genuineness of the product (Reliability), Easy accessibility to green products, Creative, innovative and modernisation features incorporated in the products, Price of the products, Quality of the products, Promotion of the products, Offers & Discounts, Product varieties available, Durability of the product (long- lasting and insurances for eco-friendly features like labelling.

Measured Consumers level of satisfaction towards green products was considered as dummy variable and run the following regression model to identify the consumers' level of perception towards green products.

Consumers' level of satisfaction towards green products $(Y1) = \beta0 + \beta1X1 + \beta2X2 + \beta3X3 + \beta4X4 + \beta5X5 + \beta6X6 + \beta7X7 + \beta8X8 + \beta9X9 + \beta10X10 + \beta11X11 + e$

Where,

    Y1= Consumers' level of satisfaction towards green products

    $\beta0$ = Intercept

    $\beta1$-$\beta11$= Slopes (estimates of coefficients)

    X_1= Availability of Green Products in the Market

    X_2= Genuineness of the Product (Reliability)

    X_3= Easy Accessibility to Green products

X_4= Creative, Innovative and Modernisation Features Incorporated in the Products

X_5= Price of the Products

X_6= Quality of the Products

X_7= Promotion of the Products

X_8= Offers & Discounts

X_9= Product Varieties Available

X_{10}= Durability of the Product (long-lasting)

X_{11}= Insurances for Eco-friendly Features like Labelling and

e = Random error, which the researcher assumed as NID for this research.

Table 4.37: Multiple Regression Model Summary Association between Consumers' Level of Perception and Satisfaction towards Green Products

R	R²	Adjusted R²	SE	F Value	Sig
.459	.210	.199	.35915	19.675	.000

Level of Significance: 5 per cent

$$Y=.1.382+.069X_1+.119X_2+.080X_3-.036X_4-.057X_5-.015X_6.030X_7+.095X_8+.035X_9+.177X_{10}-.175X_{11}$$

It has been revealed from the above econometric analysis that F ratio (19.675) is statistically significant at 5 per cent level.

This indicates that the entire regression is significant, and it establishes 45.90 per cent of relationship between the variables tested. From the above table it is seen that the coefficient of correlation (R) value .459 describes a good relationship between variables and the coefficient of determinant (R^2) .210 value establishes a significant association between the 11variables tested. Therefore the hypothesis framed stands accepted and it has been concluded that there exists a close association between consumers' level of perception towards green products and level of satisfaction towards it.

It has been found that the theoretical discussion made by Cadotte et al. (1987) and Ottman (1998) are well suited to the statistical conclusion made this section of the study. Cadotte et al. (1987) study claim that customers' satisfaction could also be defined as an evaluative response to perceived outcome of a particular consumption experience.

Ottman (1998) comments that the satisfaction is an outcome that occurs without comparing expectations. These authors' studies on customers' perception and satisfaction are closely related to each other. The following table shows the value of constant and coefficient value of each attributes to analyse the Consumers' level of satisfaction towards green products.

Table 4.38: Association between Consumers' Level of Perception and Satisfaction towards Green Products

Variables	Unstandardized Coefficients		Standardized Coefficients	t	Sig.
	B	Std. Error	Beta		
Constant	1.382	.067	-	20.609	.000
Availability of green products in the Market	.069	.028	.115	2.511	.012
Genuineness of the product (Reliability)	.119	.029	.192	4.150	.000
Easy accessibility to green products	.080	.027	.139	3.014	.003
Creative, innovative and modernisation features incorporated in the products	-.036	.029	-.054	-1.236	.217
Price of the products	-.057	.024	-.117	-2.352	.019
Quality of the products	-.015	.021	-.031	-.714	.475
Promotion of the products	-.030	.020	-.063	-1.471	.142
Offers & Discounts	.095	.022	.184	4.225	.000
Product varieties available	.035	.023	.074	1.496	.135
Durability of the product (long- lasting)	.177	.030	.347	5.939	.000
Insurances for eco-friendly features like labelling	-.175	.024	-.399	-7.178	.000

Level of Significance: 5 per cent

To determine of one or more of the independent variables are significant with the predictors and to analyse whether the consumers' level of perception towards green products and level of satisfaction towards it with the information provided above the co-efficient table is examined. Out of eleven parameters statements considered only seven were statistically significant.

The standardized co-efficient beta column reveals that the consumers' levels of satisfaction towards green products have met beta standard co-efficient ±1.382 which is statistically significant at 0.000.

Predicated Value of

Consumers' Level of Satisfaction towards Green products =

+1.382 (Constant)

+.069 (Availability of Green Products in the Market)

+.119 (Genuineness of the Product (Reliability)

+.080 (Easy Accessibility to Green products)

±.057 (Price of the Products)

+.095 (Offers & Discounts)

+.177 (Durability of the Product (Long -Lasting)

±.175 (Insurances for Eco-Friendly Features like labelling)

To assess whether consumers level of satisfaction towards green products the multiple regression modeling was performed and to the relative importance of the individual dimension of the generated scale, Multiple Regression Analysis indicated out of eleven variables tested seven variables: Availability of green Products in the Market, genuineness of the product (reliability), Easy accessibility to green products, price of the products, offers & discounts, durability of the product (long-lasting) and insurances for eco-friendly features like: labelling, these variable were found to be statistically significant.

Factor analysis technique has been applied to find the underlying dimension (factors) that exists in the eleven variables relating to the consumers' level of satisfaction towards green products.

Table 4.39: Kmo and Bartlett's Test Consumers' Level of Satisfaction towards Green Products

Kaiser-Meyer-Olkin Measure of Sampling Adequacy	.690
Bartlett's Test of Sphericity Approx. Chi-Square	3454.979
DF	55
Sig	.000

Level of Significance: 5 per cent

In the present study, Kaiser-Meyer-Olkin (KMO) Measure of Sampling Adequacy (MSA) and Bartlett's test of Sphericity were applied to verify the adequacy or appropriateness of data for factor analysis.

In this study, the value of KMO for overall matrix was found to be excellent (0.690) and Bartlett's test of Sphericity was highly significant (p<0.05).

Bartlett's Sphericity test was effective, as the chi-square value draws significance at five per cent level. The results thus indicated that the sample taken was appropriate to proceed with factor analysis procedure.

Besides Bartlett's Test of Sphericity and KMO Measure of sampling Adequacy, Communality values of all variables were also observed.

Table 4.40: Cumulative Consumers' Level of Satisfaction towards Green Products

Factors	Initial	Extraction
Availability of green products in the market	1.000	.889
Genuineness of the product (Reliability)	1.000	.748
Easy accessibility to green products	1.000	.810
Creative, innovative and modernisation features incorporated in the products	1.000	.734
Price of the products	1.000	.767
Quality of the products	1.000	.834
Promotion of the products	1.000	.723
Offers & Discounts	1.000	.802
Product varieties available	1.000	.695
Durability of the product (long- lasting)	1.000	.853
Insurances for eco-friendly features like labelling	1.000	.881

In order to provide a more parsimonious interpretation of the results, 11-item scale was then factor-analysed using the Principal Component method with Varimax rotation.

Table 4.41: Rotated Component Matrix Consumers' Level of Satisfaction towards Green Products

Factors	Factors				
	F_1	F_2	F_3	F_4	F_5
X_1 Availability of green products in the Market	-	-	-	-	.888
X_2- Genuineness of the product (Reliability)	-	.582	-	-	.551
X_3- Easy accessibility to green products	-	.845	-	-	-
X_4- Creative, innovative and modernisation features incorporated in the Products	-	.799	-	-	-
X_5- Price of the products	-	-	.731	-	-
X_6- Quality of the products	-	-	.883	-	-
X_7- Promotion of the products	-	-	-	.744	-
X_8- Offers & Discounts	-	-	-	.815	-
X_9- Product varieties available	.607	-	-	-	-
X_{10} - Durability of the product (long-lasting)	.829	-	-	-	-
X_{11}- Insurances for eco-friendly features like labelling	.882	-	-	-	-
Eigen value	2.079	1.912	1.721	1.639	1.384
% of Variance	18.898	17.385	15.646	14.899	12.585
Cumulative	18.898	36.284	51.930	66.829	79.414

Level of Significance: 5 per cent

Through an analysis of items in each factor, new dimensions were defined (Table 4.41), excluding items with a value lower than 0.5. Five factors extracted together account for 79.414 per cent of the total variance (information contained in the original 11 variables). This is good, because the researcher is able to economize on the number of variables (from 11 the researcher has reduced them to five underlying factors), while the data lost only about 20.586 per cent of the information content (79.414 per cent is retained by the five factors extracted out of the 11 original variables).

Five factors were identified as being maximum percentage variance accounted. The variables X_9, X_{10}, and X_{11} are grouped as factor I and it accounts for 18.898 per cent of the total variance. The variables X_2, X_3 and X_4 constitute the factor II and it accounts for 17.385 per cent of the total variance.

The variables X_5 and X_6 constitute the factor III and it accounts for 15.646 per cent of the total variance. The variables X_7 and X_8 constitute the factor IV and it accounts for 14.899 per cent of the total variance.

The variables X_1 and X_2, constitute the factor V and it accounts for 12.585 per cent of the total variance.

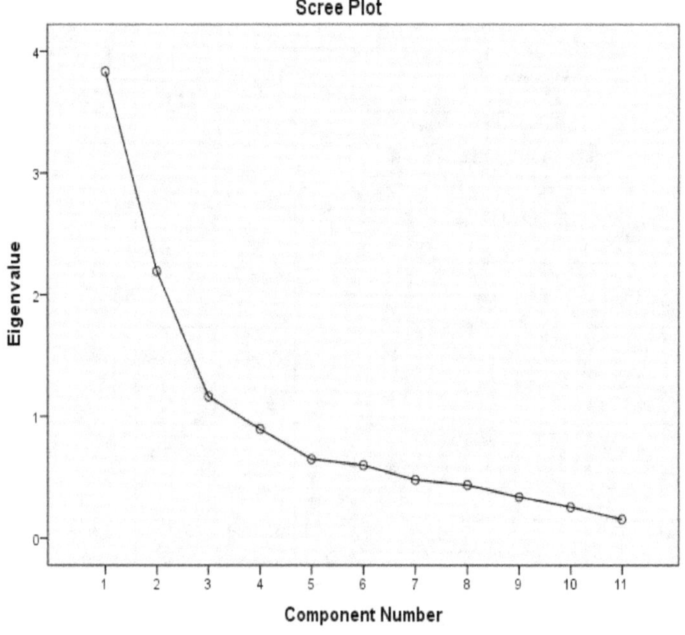

Exhibit 4.10: Scree Plot Consumers' Level of Satisfaction towards Green Products

A Scree plot is a graph that plots the total variance associated with each factor. It is a visual display of how many factors there are in the data. The Scree plot graphs the Eigenvalue against the factor number. It has been observed that although there are 11 principal components only 4 factors have Eigenvalues over one. So it can expect three principal components in the data. The curve indicates the inflexion on the curve.

Table 4.42: Summary of Rotation Factor Analysis & Cronbach's Alpha Consumers' Level of Satisfaction towards Green Products

Factors	Factor Interpretation	Variables included in the factors	Cronbach's Alpha
F_1	Highly Satisfied	Product varieties available, durability of the product (long-lasting), Insurances for eco-friendly features like labelling.	.869
F_2	Satisfied	Genuineness of the product (Reliability), easy accessibility to green products, creative, innovative and modernisation features incorporated in the products	.780
F_3	Moderately Satisfied	Price of the products, quality of the products.	.676
F_4	Dissatisfied	Promotion of the products offers & discounts.	.649
F_5	Highly Dissatisfied	Availability of green products in the market and genuineness of the product (Reliability).	.605

Source: Computed From Primary Data

The internal consistency of each factor was estimated individually using the alpha coefficient of Cronbach's (α). Factor analysis was applied to establish and reveal the correlation between consumers' level of satisfaction towards green products. The Cronbach's reliability values of .869, .780, .676, .649, and .605 indicate significant correlation between the variables tested and a good internal consistency.

4.1.6. *Consumers' Belief on Benefits of Buying Green Products*

Green consumption is normally related to environmentally responsible consumption where consumers consider the environmental impact of purchasing, using, and disposing of various products, or using various green services.

Generally consumers accepted to buy green products when their primary need for performance, quality, convenience, and affordability were met, and when they understood how a green product could help them in solving environmental issues, that is currently prevalent across the globe.

This section of analysis draws discussion on the nature of benefits realised by the consumers due to the usage of green products. It is discussed in tables 4.43 to 4.65.

Table 4.43: Consumers' Level of Agreeability about Benefits Received by Buying Green Products

Agreeability	Strong Agree	Agree	Moderate	Disagree	Strongly Disagree	Sum	Mean	Rank
Green products ensure healthy lifestyle	190 (25.33)	516 (68.80)	44 (5.87)	0 (0.00)	0 (0.00)	3146	4.19	2
Green products help to maintain a healthy home and family	186 (24.80)	528 (70.40)	36 (4.80)	0 (0.00)	0 (0.00)	3150	4.20	1
Green products prevent us from using harmful chemicals	158 (21.07)	431 (57.47)	151 (20.13)	10 (1.33)	0 (0.00)	2987	3.98	4
Green products are risk free products (both on human and on environment)	100 (13.33)	413 (55.07)	237 (31.60)	0 (0.00)	0 (0.00)	2863	3.82	6
Green products are price-wise reasonable	86 (11.47)	305 (40.67)	277 (36.93)	82 (10.93)	0 (0.00)	2645	3.53	10
Green products are reusable	67 (8.93)	409 (54.53)	198 (26.40)	76 (10.13)	0 (0.00)	2717	3.62	9
Green products ensure energy efficiency and save scarce resources	134 (17.87)	333 (44.40)	198 (26.40)	85 (11.33)	0 (0.00)	2766	3.69	8
Green products ensure sustainability of modern earth	151 (20.13)	327 (43.60)	229 (30.53)	43 (5.73)	0 (0.00)	2836	3.78	7
Green products gives us freedom from the guilty feeling of harming environment	164 (21.87)	350 (46.67)	201 (26.80)	35 (44..67)	0 (0.00)	2893	3.86	5
Now-a-days there are innumerable, products in the market in the name of green products	307 (40.93)	295 (39.33)	113 (15.07)	35 (4.67)	0 (0.00)	3124	4.17	3

Source: Primary Data

There are a number of benefits the consumers reap due to the usage of green products. As per the survey results, majority of the consumers have benefited from having healthy home and family and conversion to health lifestyles, due to consumption of green products. These two variables are ranked in the first and second places with the highest mean score of 4.20 and 4.19, respectively. Factors like a) available of more fashionable green products in the market in recent times, b) aims to prevent self and family from harmful chemicals and c) feel of freedom from the guilt feel of harming environment have motivated majority of consumers to buy green products, which they gratefully registered as the major benefits derived by them due to the active consumption of green products. These factors are ranked in third, fourth and fifth places with the mean score of 4.17, 3.98 and 3.86 respectively. The benefits realised by the consumers like: risk-free products (both on human and on environment), green products ensure sustainability of modern earth, green products ensuring energy efficiency and saving scare resources, green products ensure reusability of products and benefitted from economic pricing factors are ranked in sixth, seventh, eighth, ninth and tenth places with the mean score of 3.82, 3.78, 3.69, 3.62 and 3.53 respectively.

Thus it has been concluded that majority of the consumers have benefited from having a healthy home and family and conversion to health life-styles, due to consumption of green products. The consumers living across Coimbatore city are slowly turning towards buying green products, although the proportionate number of buyers is less as discussed in the Table: 4.19, i.e., only 40.80 per cent of the consumers surveyed in Coimbatore city always prefer buying green products.

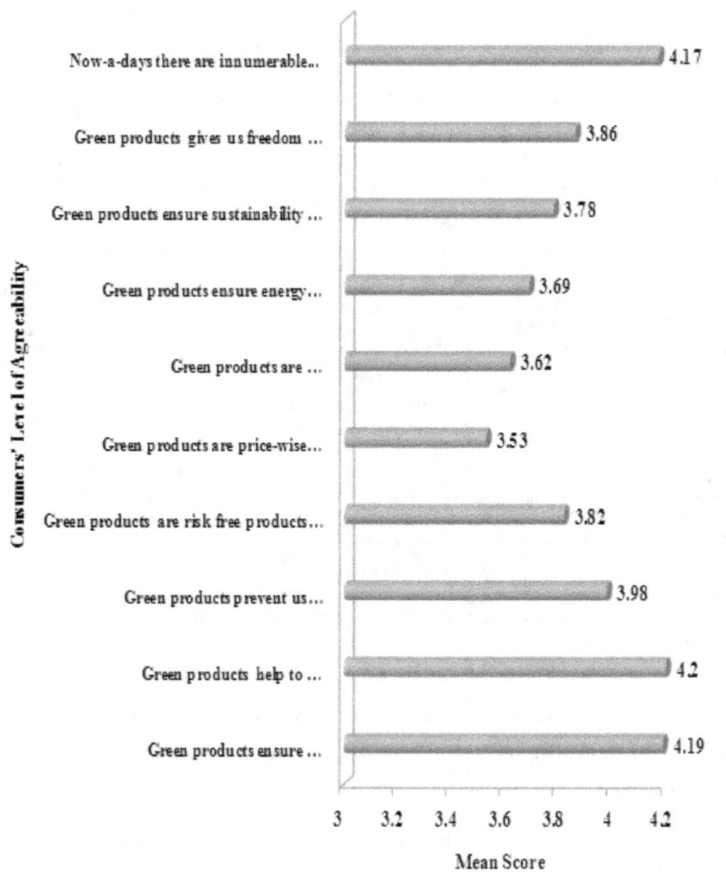

Exhibit 4.11: Consumers' Level of Agreeability about Benefits Obtained by Buying Green Products

Takafumi (2002) stated that green products can provide direct and indirect value to consumers. Direct value means the value will give immediate effect to consumers such as increase in safety or reduction in capital if consumers use green products. Whereas, indirect value means that consumers believe that utilizing green products will benefit and protect the environment although they cannot determine the immediate benefits from utilizing the green products.

In relation to the above study, Walter (1990) had found that consumers' concern on environmental issues does not always translate into purchasing decisions. Similarly, Ahmed et al. (2001) claimed that different segments of the consumers react differently towards the green issues. Drawing empirical evidences from these studies the following hypothesis is framed and tested.

H7: Consumers' level of agreeability about benefits obtained by buying green products varies among their demographic and socio–economic status.

Table 4.44: Measure of Dispersion Consumers' Level of Agreeability about Benefits Obtained by Buying Green Products Vs their Gender

Variables	Male		Female	
	Mean	SD	Mean	SD
Green products ensure healthy lifestyle	1.85	.537	1.77	.511
Green products help to maintain a healthy home and family	1.94	.416	1.68	.542
Green products prevent us from using harmful chemicals	2.23	.598	1.84	.697
Green products are risk free products (both on human and on environment)	2.25	.643	2.13	.643
Green products are price-wise reasonable	2.44	.848	2.50	.826
Green products are reusable	2.52	.733	2.26	.809
Green products ensure energy efficiency and save scarce resources	2.39	.814	2.25	.951
Green products ensure sustainability of modern earth	2.12	.733	2.30	.895
Green products gives us freedom from the guilty feeling of harming environment	2.49	.753	1.86	.742
Now-a-days there are innumerable, products in the market in the name of green products	2.06	.989	1.65	.661

Level of Significance: 5 per cent

The measure of dispersion depicted in the above table reveals that the level of agreeability about benefits obtained by buying green products varies among the male and female consumers surveyed for the study.

The first hypothesis of the study claims that women are more knowledgeable about green products when compared to their male counterparts. Since, females were more conscious than males in protecting the environment they always focus on the issues that ensure sustainability of modern earth.

Table 4.45: Result of Anova Consumers' Level of Agreeability about Benefits Obtained by Buying Green Products Vs their Gender

Variables	Source	Sum of Square	DF	Mean Square	F	Sig
Green products ensure healthy lifestyle	Between Groups	1.280	1	1.280	4.687	.031
	Within Groups	204.299	748	.273		
	Total	205.579	749	-		
Green products help to maintain a healthy home and family	Between Groups	12.526	1	12.526	52.205	.000
	Within Groups	179.474	748	.240		
	Total	192.000	749	-		
Green products prevent us from using harmful chemicals	Between Groups	28.087	1	28.087	65.513	.000
	Within Groups	320.688	748	.429		
	Total	348.775	749	-		
Green products are risk free products (both on human and on environment)	Between Groups	2.521	1	2.521	6.094	.014
	Within Groups	309.454	748	.414		
	Total	311.975	749	-		
Green products are price-wise reasonable	Between Groups	.782	1	.782	1.120	.290
	Within Groups	522.185	748	.698		
	Total	522.967	749	-		
Green products are reusable	Between Groups	12.020	1	12.020	19.971	.000
	Within Groups	450.195	748	.602		
	Total	462.215	749	-		
Green products ensure energy efficiency and save scarce resources	Between Groups	3.415	1	3.415	4.289	.039
	Within Groups	595.577	748	.796		
	Total	598.992	749	-		
Green products ensure sustainability of modern earth	Between Groups	5.685	1	5.685	8.331	.004
	Within Groups	510.454	748	.682		
	Total	516.139	749	-		
Green products gives us freedom from the guilty feeling of harming environment	Between Groups	72.630	1	72.630	130.249	.000
	Within Groups	417.105	748	.558		
	Total	489.735	749	-		
Now-a-days there are innumerable, products in the market in the name of green products	Between Groups	31.596	1	31.596	46.532	.000
	Within Groups	507.902	748	.679		
	Total	539.499	749	-		

Level of Significance: 5 per cent

From the above table it has been inferred that probability value of ANOVA at 5 per cent level does establish a good relationship between the variables tested. Therefore, the hypothesis framed stands accepted and it has been concluded that consumers' level of agreeability about benefits obtained by buying green products varies among gender groups surveyed. However it is exceptional in the case of benefits received from economic pricing.

Table 4.46: Consumers' Level of Agreeability About Benefits Obtained by Buying Green Products Vs their Age

Variables	25-30-Years		31-35-Years		36-40-Years		Above-40-Years	
	Mean	SD	Mean	SD	Mean	SD	Mean	SD
Green products ensure healthy lifestyle	1.50	.631	2.02	.512	1.96	.197	1.77	.440
Green products help to maintain a healthy home and family	1.43	.523	2.02	.442	1.86	.349	1.99	.435
Green products prevent us from using harmful chemicals	1.83	.748	2.03	.502	2.10	.765	2.19	.599
Green products are risk free products (both on human and on environment)	2.04	.606	2.28	.615	2.27	.529	2.14	.833
Green products are price-wise reasonable	2.30	.671	2.61	.820	2.63	.854	2.34	.985
Green products are reusable	2.37	.626	2.43	.919	2.52	.881	2.11	.575
Green products ensure energy efficiency and save scarce resources	2.07	1.016	2.67	.783	2.28	.905	2.23	.631
Green products ensure sustainability of modern earth	2.22	.826	2.51	.749	1.90	.732	2.26	.923
Green products gives us freedom from the guilty feeling of harming environment	1.66	.654	2.26	.655	2.36	.926	2.43	.714
Now-a-days there are innumerable, products in the market in the name of green products	1.54	.518	1.96	.840	2.02	1.022	1.86	.892

Level of Significance: 5 per cent

Above presented mean score analysis indicates that consumers at the age group of 31-35 years are more conscious about green products and its usability in comparison to the other age category of consumers.

The study indicates that age of the consumers has a direct relationship with their understanding and agreeability towards the benefits of the green products.

Table 4.47: Result of Anova Consumers' Level of Agreeability about Benefits Obtained by Buying Green Products Vs their Age

Variables	Source	Sum of Square	DF	Mean Square	F	Sig
Green products ensure healthy lifestyle	Between Groups	33.867	3	11.289	49.044	.000
	Within Groups	171.712	746	.230		
	Total	205.579	749	-		
Green products help to maintain a healthy home and family	Between Groups	44.583	3	14.861	75.203	.000
	Within Groups	147.417	746	.198		
	Total	192.000	749	-		
Green products prevent us from using harmful chemicals	Between Groups	13.435	3	4.478	9.963	.000
	Within Groups	335.339	746	.450		
	Total	348.775	749	-		
Green products are risk free products (both on human and on environment)	Between Groups	8.333	3	2.778	6.824	.000
	Within Groups	303.642	746	.407		
	Total	311.975	749	-		
Green products are price-wise reasonable	Between Groups	17.277	3	5.759	8.496	.000
	Within Groups	505.689	746	.678		
	Total	522.967	749	-		
Green products are reusable	Between Groups	14.621	3	4.874	8.123	.000
	Within Groups	447.593	746	.600		
	Total	462.215	749	-		
Green products ensure energy efficiency and save scarce resources	Between Groups	39.208	3	13.069	17.417	.000
	Within Groups	559.784	746	.750		
	Total	598.992	749	-		
Green products ensure sustainability of modern earth	Between Groups	36.815	3	12.272	19.099	.000
	Within Groups	479.323	746	.643		
	Total	516.139	749	-		
Green products gives us freedom from the guilty feeling of harming environment	Between Groups	74.093	3	24.698	44.328	.000
	Within Groups	415.642	746	.557		
	Total	489.735	749	-		
Now-a-days there are innumerable, products in the market in the name of green products	Between Groups	28.565	3	9.522	13.902	.000
	Within Groups	510.933	746	.685		
	Total	539.499	749	-		

Level of Significance: 5 per cent

From the above table it has been inferred that probability value of ANOVA at 5 per cent level does establish a good relationship between the variables tested.

Therefore, the hypothesis framed stands accepted and it has been concluded that consumers' level of agreeability about benefits obtained by buying green products varies among different age groups of population surveyed.

Table 4.48: Consumers' Level of Agreeability about Benefits Obtained by Buying Green Products Vs their Marital Status

Variables	Married		Unmarried		Others	
	Mean	SD	Mean	SD	Mean	SD
Green products ensure healthy lifestyle	1.85	.477	1.65	.645	1.00	000
Green products help to maintain a healthy home and family	1.87	.479	1.55	.523	1.00	000
Green products prevent us from using harmful chemicals	2.03	.656	1.97	.770	1.00	000
Green products are risk free products (both on human and on environment)	2.24	.654	1.98	.564	1.00	000
Green products are price-wise reasonable	2.55	.877	2.20	.582	1.00	000
Green products are reusable	2.30	.810	2.67	.610	2.00	000
Green products ensure energy efficiency and save scarce resources	2.26	.856	2.50	1.007	2.00	000
Green products ensure sustainability of modern earth	2.21	.810	2.24	.900	1.00	000
Green products gives us freedom from the guilty feeling of harming environment	2.25	.813	1.76	.666	1.00	000
Now-a-days there are innumerable, products in the market in the name of green products	1.93	.897	1.48	.501	1.00	000

Level of Significance: 5 per cent

The measure of dispersion indicated that consumers' level of agreeability about benefits obtained by buying green products differ among married and unmarried respondents surveyed.

It has been observed that married consumers are more knowledgeable about the benefits of green products in comparison to the unmarried youth.

Table 4.49: Result of Anova Consumers' Level of Agreeability about Benefits Obtained by Buying Green Products Vs their Marital Status

Variables	Source	Sum of Square	DF	Mean Square	F	Sig
Green products ensure healthy lifestyle	Between Groups	5.528	2	2.764	10.321	.000
	Within Groups	200.051	747	.268		
	Total	205.579	749	-		
Green products help to maintain a healthy home and family	Between Groups	13.282	2	6.641	27.758	.000
	Within Groups	178.718	747	.239		
	Total	192.000	749	-		
Green products prevent us from using harmful chemicals	Between Groups	1.544	2	.772	1.661	.191
	Within Groups	347.231	747	.465		
	Total	348.775	749	-		
Green products are risk free products (both on human and on environment)	Between Groups	9.842	2	4.921	12.167	.000
	Within Groups	302.133	747	.404		
	Total	311.975	749	-		
Green products are price-wise reasonable	Between Groups	17.161	2	8.580	12.672	.000
	Within Groups	505.806	747	.677		
	Total	522.967	749	-		
Green products are reusable	Between Groups	17.745	2	8.873	14.912	.000
	Within Groups	444.469	747	.595		
	Total	462.215	749	-		
Green products ensure energy efficiency and save scarce resources	Between Groups	7.077	2	3.538	4.466	.012
	Within Groups	591.915	747	.792		
	Total	598.992	749	-		
Green products ensure sustainability of modern earth	Between Groups	1.586	2	.793	1.151	.317
	Within Groups	514.553	747	.689		
	Total	516.139	749	-		
Green products gives us freedom from the guilty feeling of harming environment	Between Groups	30.955	2	15.478	25.201	.000
	Within Groups	458.779	747	.614		
	Total	489.735	749	-		
Now-a-days there are innumerable, products in the market in the name of green products	Between Groups	26.911	2	13.456	19.609	.000
	Within Groups	512.587	747	.686		
	Total	539.499	749	-		

Level of Significance: 5 per cent

From the above table it has been inferred that probability value of ANOVA at 5 per cent level does establish a good relationship between the variables tested. Therefore, the hypothesis framed stands accepted and it has been concluded that consumers' level of agreeability about benefits obtained by buying green products differ among married and unmarried respondents surveyed.

It is exceptional in the case of the variables like: prevention from usage of harmful chemical and ensure sustainability of mother earth.

Table 4.50: Consumers' Level of Agreeability about Benefits Obtained by Buying Green Products Vs their Educational Qualification

Variables	School Level		UG		PG		Others	
	Mean	SD	Mean	SD	Mean	SD	Mean	SD
Green products ensure healthy lifestyle	1.69	.562	1.70	.459	2.16	.503	1.76	.440
Green products help to maintain a healthy home and family	1.72	.551	1.68	.585	1.94	.263	1.93	.438
Green products prevent us from using harmful chemicals	2.02	.625	1.70	.512	2.28	.517	2.22	.883
Green products are risk free products (both on human and on environment)	2.43	.507	2.16	.629	2.11	.468	1.98	.834
Green products are price-wise reasonable	2.67	.911	2.34	.774	2.17	.549	2.70	.918
Green products are reusable	2.31	.763	2.44	.754	2.22	.517	2.51	1.001
Green products ensure energy efficiency and save scarce resources	2.25	.927	2.28	.938	2.30	.708	2.44	.938
Green products ensure sustainability of modern earth	2.57	.789	2.30	.777	2.14	.610	1.77	.906
Green products gives us freedom from the guilty feeling of harming environment	2.22	.734	1.77	.621	2.00	.651	2.69	.927
Now-a-days there are innumerable, products in the market in the name of green products	1.99	.740	1.62	.626	1.76	.668	2.01	1.227

Level of Significance: 5 per cent

The above presented data analysis reveals that respondents' educational level has a significant impact on their green purchase intention.

It indicates that the consumers' green purchase intention is getting lower with low education level, that is, post-graduate respondents have more favourable attitude towards green purchase intention and benefits related to it as compared to those respondents with lower level of education.

Table 4.51: Result of Anova Consumers' Level of Agreeability about Benefits Obtained by Buying Green Products Vs their Educational Qualification

Variables	Source	Sum of Square	DF	Mean Square	F	Sig
Green products ensure healthy lifestyle	Between Groups	24.239	3	8.080	33.238	.000
	Within Groups	181.340	746	.243		
	Total	205.579	749	-		
Green products help to maintain a healthy home and family	Between Groups	10.877	3	3.626	14.934	.000
	Within Groups	181.123	746	.243		
	Total	192.000	749	-		
Green products prevent us from using harmful chemicals	Between Groups	40.136	3	13.379	32.337	.000
	Within Groups	308.638	746	.414		
	Total	348.775	749	-		
Green products are risk free products (both on human and on environment)	Between Groups	20.209	3	6.736	17.224	.000
	Within Groups	291.765	746	.391		
	Total	311.975	749	-		
Green products are price-wise reasonable	Between Groups	34.481	3	11.494	17.553	.000
	Within Groups	488.486	746	.655		
	Total	522.967	749	-		
Green products are reusable	Between Groups	8.158	3	2.719	4.468	.004
	Within Groups	454.057	746	.609		
	Total	462.215	749	-		
Green products ensure energy efficiency and save scarce resources	Between Groups	3.956	3	1.319	1.653	.176
	Within Groups	595.036	746	.798		
	Total	598.992	749	-		
Green products ensure sustainability of modern earth	Between Groups	60.606	3	20.202	33.083	.000
	Within Groups	455.533	746	.611		
	Total	516.139	749	-		
Green products gives us freedom from the guilty feeling of harming environment	Between Groups	86.294	3	28.765	53.189	.000
	Within Groups	403.441	746	.541		
	Total	489.735	749	-		
Now-a-days there are innumerable, products in the market in the name of green products	Between Groups	20.817	3	6.939	9.980	.000
	Within Groups	518.681	746	.695		
	Total	539.499	749	-		

Level of Significance: 5 per cent

From the above table it has been inferred that probability value of ANOVA at 5 per cent level does establish a good relationship between the variables tested. Therefore, the hypothesis framed stands accepted and it has been concluded that consumers' level of agreeability about benefits obtained by buying green products differ among various levels of educated consumers. However it is exceptional in the case of ensuring energy efficiency and saving scarce resources.

Table 4.52: Consumers' Level of Agreeability about Benefits Obtained by Buying Green Products Vs their Occupational Status

Variables	Agriculturist		Self-Employed		Professional		Employee		Others	
	Mean	SD	Mean	SD	Mean	SD	Mean	SD	Mean	SD
Green products ensure healthy lifestyle	1.64	.624	1.82	.401	1.84	.738	1.92	.313	1.75	.447
Green products help to maintain a healthy home and family	1.57	.516	1.88	.484	1.64	.481	2.03	.351	1.80	.562
Green products prevent us from using harmful chemicals	1.75	.479	2.41	.739	1.57	.591	2.01	.477	2.18	.647
Green products are risk free products (both on human and on environment)	2.25	.479	1.92	.712	1.92	.656	2.32	.497	2.58	.508
Green products are price-wise reasonable	2.55	.519	2.67	.585	2.04	.715	2.52	.881	2.58	1.130
Green products are reusable	2.11	.368	2.45	.624	2.04	.823	2.40	.860	2.78	.840
Green products ensure energy efficiency and save scarce resources	1.75	.776	2.44	.648	2.15	.696	2.32	.981	2.70	1.075
Green products ensure sustainability of modern earth	2.22	.418	2.04	.794	2.11	.764	2.39	.971	2.38	.935
Green products gives us freedom from the guilty feeling of harming environment	1.74	.610	2.39	.642	1.73	.654	2.35	.748	2.33	1.012
Now-a-days there are innumerable, products in the market in the name of green products	1.90	.603	1.75	.861	1.52	.636	1.88	.859	2.16	1.013

Level of Significance: 5 per cent

The above presented data analysis indicates consumers' level of agreeability about benefits obtained by buying green products differ among different occupational groups.

Table 4.53: Result of Anova Consumers' Level of Agreeability about Benefits Obtained by Buying Green Products Vs their Occupational Status

Variables	Source	Sum of Square	DF	Mean Square	F	Sig
Green products ensure healthy lifestyle	Between Groups	5.521	4	1.380	5.140	.000
	Within Groups	200.057	745	.269		
	Total	205.579	749	-		
Green products help to maintain a healthy home and family	Between Groups	17.963	4	4.491	19.224	.000
	Within Groups	174.037	745	.234		
	Total	192.000	749	-		
Green products prevent us from using harmful chemicals	Between Groups	71.314	4	17.828	47.870	.000
	Within Groups	277.461	745	.372		
	Total	348.775	749	-		
Green products are risk free products (both on human and on environment)	Between Groups	51.206	4	12.802	36.573	.000
	Within Groups	260.768	745	.350		
	Total	311.975	749	-		
Green products are price-wise reasonable	Between Groups	39.538	4	9.884	15.233	.000
	Within Groups	483.429	745	.649		
	Total	522.967	749	-		
Green products are reusable	Between Groups	52.815	4	13.204	24.028	.000
	Within Groups	409.399	745	.550		
	Total	462.215	749	-		
Green products ensure energy efficiency and save scarce resources	Between Groups	63.274	4	15.819	21.998	.000
	Within Groups	535.718	745	.719		
	Total	598.992	749	-		
Green products ensure sustainability of modern earth	Between Groups	16.417	4	4.104	6.119	.000
	Within Groups	499.722	745	.671		
	Total	516.139	749	-		
Green products gives us freedom from the guilty feeling of harming environment	Between Groups	66.628	4	16.657	29.329	.000
	Within Groups	423.107	745	.568		
	Total	489.735	749	-		
Now-a-days there are innumerable, products in the market in the name of green products	Between Groups	34.109	4	8.527	12.570	.000
	Within Groups	505.390	745	.678		
	Total	539.499	749	-		

Level of Significance: 5 per cent

From the above table it has been inferred that probability value of ANOVA at 5 per cent level does establish a good relationship between the variables tested. Therefore, the hypothesis framed stands accepted and it has been concluded that consumers' level of agreeability about benefits obtained by buying green products differ among different occupational groups.

Table 4.54: Consumers' Level of Agreeability about Benefits Obtained by Buying Green Products Vs their Monthly Income

Variables	Less than Rs.10.000		Rs.10,001 to 20,000		Rs.20,001 to Rs.30,000		Rs.30,001 to Rs.40,000		Rs.40,001 & Above	
	Mean	SD	Mean	SD	Mean	SD	Mean	SD	Mean	SD
Green products ensure healthy lifestyle	1.72	.548	1.74	.632	2.03	.256	1.76	.432	3.00	000
Green products help to maintain a healthy home and family	1.67	.565	1.77	.432	1.98	.408	1.95	.494	1.00	000
Green products prevent us from using harmful chemicals	1.78	.680	1.96	.588	2.48	.638	1.98	.471	2.00	000
Green products are risk free products (both on human and on environment)	2.22	.615	2.02	.730	2.34	.579	2.11	.588	2.00	000
Green products are price-wise reasonable	2.52	.831	2.36	.865	2.73	.822	2.04	.532	1.00	000
Green products are reusable	2.22	.770	2.33	.778	2.83	.781	2.04	.331	3.00	000
Green products ensure energy efficiency and save scarce resources	2.32	1.001	1.84	.675	2.91	.709	2.09	.450	2.00	000
Green products ensure sustainability of modern earth	2.34	.991	2.15	.771	2.03	.657	2.35	.553	2.00	000
Green products gives us freedom from the guilty feeling of harming environment	1.96	.768	2.10	.818	2.37	.876	2.40	.563	2.00	000
Now-a-days there are innumerable, products in the market in the name of green products	1.56	.609	1.74	.850	2.44	.985	1.72	.573	2.00	000

Level of Significance: 5 per cent

It has been inferred from the above presented data analysis that consumers with higher income clearly have more understanding on the benefits of the green products in comparison to the low income category of consumers.

Table 4.55: Result of Anova Consumers' Level of Agreeability about Benefits Obtained by Buying Green Products Vs their Monthly Income

Variables	Source	Sum of Square	DF	Mean Square	F	Sig
Green products ensure healthy lifestyle	Between Groups	14.135	4	3.534	13.751	.000
	Within Groups	191.444	745	.257		
	Total	205.579	749	-		
Green products help to maintain a healthy home and family	Between Groups	13.486	4	3.371	14.070	.000
	Within Groups	178.514	745	.240		
	Total	192.000	749	-		
Green products prevent us from using harmful chemicals	Between Groups	56.363	4	14.091	35.900	.000
	Within Groups	292.412	745	.392		
	Total	348.775	749	-		
Green products are risk free products (both on human and on environment)	Between Groups	10.594	4	2.649	6.547	.000
	Within Groups	301.380	745	.405		
	Total	311.975	749	-		
Green products are price-wise reasonable	Between Groups	33.006	4	8.252	12.547	.000
	Within Groups	489.961	745	.658		
	Total	522.967	749	-		
Green products are reusable	Between Groups	54.216	4	13.554	24.750	.000
	Within Groups	407.998	745	.548		
	Total	462.215	749	-		
Green products ensure energy efficiency and save scarce resources	Between Groups	112.577	4	28.144	43.106	.000
	Within Groups	486.415	745	.653		
	Total	598.992	749	-		
Green products ensure sustainability of modern earth	Between Groups	13.175	4	3.294	4.879	.001
	Within Groups	502.963	745	.675		
	Total	516.139	749	-		
Green products gives us freedom from the guilty feeling of harming environment	Between Groups	25.170	4	6.293	10.091	.000
	Within Groups	464.564	745	.624		
	Total	489.735	749	-		
Now-a-days there are innumerable, products in the market in the name of green products	Between Groups	90.827	4	22.707	37.704	.000
	Within Groups	448.671	745	.602		
	Total	539.499	749	-		

Level of Significance: 5 per cent

From the above table it has been inferred that probability value of ANOVA at 5 per cent level does establish a good relationship between the variables tested. Therefore, the hypothesis framed stands accepted and it has been concluded that consumers' level of agreeability about benefits obtained by buying green products differ among income category of sample population.

Table 4.56: Consumers' Level of Agreeability about Benefits Obtained by Buying Green Products Vs their Family Type

Variables	Joint		Nuclear	
	Mean	SD	Mean	SD
Green products ensure healthy lifestyle	1.74	.450	1.86	.577
Green products help to maintain a healthy home and family	1.82	.471	1.78	.536
Green products prevent us from using harmful chemicals	2.10	.586	1.94	.752
Green products are risk free products (both on human and on environment)	2.19	.695	2.17	.598
Green products are price-wise reasonable	2.63	.993	2.34	.634
Green products are reusable	2.80	.773	2.00	.579
Green products ensure energy efficiency and save scarce resources	2.65	.904	2.01	.772
Green products ensure sustainability of modern earth	2.55	.914	1.92	.605
Green products gives us freedom from the guilty feeling of harming environment	2.38	.899	1.93	.647
Now-a-days there are innumerable, products in the market in the name of green products	1.90	.966	1.78	.724

Level of Significance: 5 per cent

The statistical data presented in the above table indicates that joint families have well understood the benefits of green products in comparison to the nuclear families.

Table 4.57: Result of Anova Consumers' Level of Agreeability about Benefits Obtained by Buying Green Products Vs their Family Type

Variables	Source	Sum of Square	DF	Mean Square	F	Sig
Green products ensure healthy lifestyle	Between Groups	2.564	1	2.564	9.446	.002
	Within Groups	203.015	748	.271		
	Total	205.579	749	-		
Green products help to maintain a healthy home and family	Between Groups	.262	1	.262	1.022	.312
	Within Groups	191.738	748	.256		
	Total	192.000	749	-		
Green products prevent us from using harmful chemicals	Between Groups	4.451	1	4.451	9.669	.002
	Within Groups	344.324	748	.460		
	Total	348.775	749	-		
Green products are risk free products (both on human and on environment)	Between Groups	.053	1	.053	.128	.721
	Within Groups	311.921	748	.417		
	Total	311.975	749	-		
Green products are price-wise reasonable	Between Groups	15.577	1	15.577	22.964	.000
	Within Groups	507.390	748	.678		
	Total	522.967	749	-		
Green products are reusable	Between	118.817	1	118.817		

Variables	Source	Sum of Square	DF	Mean Square	F	Sig
	Groups				258.812	.000
	Within Groups	343.397	748	.459		
	Total	462.215	749	-		
Green products ensure energy efficiency and save scarce resources	Between Groups	74.776	1	74.776	106.698	.000
	Within Groups	524.216	748	.701		
	Total	598.992	749	-		
Green products ensure sustainability of modern earth	Between Groups	76.217	1	76.217	129.591	.000
	Within Groups	439.922	748	.588		
	Total	516.139	749	-		
Green products gives us freedom from the guilty feeling of harming environment	Between Groups	38.965	1	38.965	64.658	.000
	Within Groups	450.769	748	.603		
	Total	489.735	749	-		
Now-a-days there are innumerable, products in the market in the name of green products	Between Groups	2.754	1	2.754	3.839	.050
	Within Groups	536.744	748	.718		
	Total	539.499	749	-		

Level of Significance: 5 per cent

From the above table it has been inferred that probability value of ANOVA at 5 per cent level does establish a good relationship between the variables tested. Therefore, the hypothesis framed stands accepted and it has been concluded that consumers' level of agreeability about benefits obtained by buying green products differ among family types. However, it is exceptional in the case of gain of healthy home and family and risk free products both on human and on environment.

Table 4.58: Consumers' Level of Agreeability about Benefits Obtained by Buying Green Products Vs their Family Size

Variables	Two Members		Three Members		Four Members		Above 4 Members	
	Mean	SD	Mean	SD	Mean	SD	Mean	SD
Green products ensure healthy lifestyle	1.71	.846	1.56	.498	1.91	.479	1.83	.392
Green products help to maintain a healthy home and family	1.74	.443	1.57	.513	1.80	.549	1.97	.381
Green products prevent us from using harmful chemicals	2.24	.513	1.66	.608	2.00	.758	2.19	.552
Green products are risk free products (both on human and on environment)	2.00	.783	2.18	.736	2.21	.577	2.21	.628
Green products are price-wise reasonable	2.45	.575	2.47	.813	2.52	.759	2.42	1.023
Green products are reusable	2.33	.551	2.11	.592	2.35	.818	2.59	.851
Green products ensure energy efficiency and save scarce resources	1.96	.642	1.87	.777	2.55	.942	2.34	.823
Green products ensure sustainability of modern earth	1.83	.755	2.16	.649	2.30	.932	2.26	.742
Green products gives us freedom from the guilty feeling of harming environment	2.17	.598	1.76	.771	2.14	.743	2.36	.909
Now-a-days there are innumerable, products in the market in the name of green products	1.38	.489	1.87	.767	1.71	.737	2.17	1.023

Level of Significance: 5 per cent

As observed in the above-mentioned demographic and socio-economic variable, family size of the consumers significantly influence their level of understanding the benefits of green products.

Table 4.59: Result of Anovaconsumers' Level of Agreeability about Benefits Obtained by Buying Green Products Vs their Family Size

Variables	Source	Sum of Square	DF	Mean Square	F	Sig
Green products ensure healthy lifestyle	Between Groups	11.760	3	3.920	15.088	.000
	Within Groups	193.818	746	.260		
	Total	205.579	749	-		
Green products help to maintain a healthy home and family	Between Groups	13.012	3	4.337	18.077	.000
	Within Groups	178.988	746	.240		
	Total	192.000	749	-		
Green products prevent us from using harmful chemicals	Between Groups	26.678	3	8.893	20.596	.000
	Within Groups	322.097	746	.432		
	Total	348.775	749	-		
Green products are risk free products (both on human and on environment)	Between Groups	2.912	3	.971	2.343	.072
	Within Groups	309.063	746	.414		
	Total	311.975	749	-		
Green products are price-wise reasonable	Between Groups	1.331	3	.444	.634	.593
	Within Groups	521.636	746	.699		
	Total	522.967	749	-		
Green products are reusable	Between Groups	19.319	3	6.440	10.847	.000
	Within Groups	442.896	746	.594		
	Total	462.215	749	-		
Green products ensure energy efficiency and save scarce resources	Between Groups	53.178	3	17.726	24.227	.000
	Within Groups	545.814	746	.732		
	Total	598.992	749			
Green products ensure sustainability of modern earth	Between Groups	14.643	3	4.881	7.261	.000
	Within Groups	501.495	746	.672		
	Total	516.139	749	-		
Green products gives us freedom from the guilty feeling of harming environment	Between Groups	29.221	3	9.740	15.779	.000
	Within Groups	460.514	746	.617		
	Total	489.735	749	-		
Now-a-days there are innumerable, products in the market in the name of green products	Between Groups	44.582	3	14.861	22.400	.000
	Within Groups	494.916	746	.663		
	Total	539.499	749	-		

Level of Significance: 5 per cent

From the above table it has been inferred that probability value of ANOVA at 5 per cent level does establish a good relationship between the variables tested. Therefore, the hypothesis framed stands accepted and it has been concluded that consumers' level of agreeability about benefits obtained by buying green products differ based on their family size. The hypothesis framed stands rejected in the case of consumers' realisation on risk-free products (both on human and on environment.

Table 4.60: Consumers' Level of Agreeability about Benefits Obtained by Buying Green Products Vs their Family Income

Variables	Single Income		Dual Income	
	Mean	SD	Mean	SD
Green products ensure healthy lifestyle	1.78	.471	1.83	.569
Green products help to maintain a healthy home and family	1.84	.518	1.76	.493
Green products prevent us from using harmful chemicals	2.13	.665	1.91	.681
Green products are risk free products (both on human and on environment)	2.26	.613	2.11	.667
Green products are price-wise reasonable	2.63	.873	2.32	.770
Green products are reusable	2.56	.767	2.20	.763
Green products ensure energy efficiency and save scarce resources	2.58	.892	2.06	.820
Green products ensure sustainability of modern earth	2.40	.914	2.05	.704
Green products gives us freedom from the guilty feeling of harming environment	2.37	.824	1.93	.733
Now-a-days there are innumerable, products in the market in the name of green products	1.99	.958	1.69	.701

Level of Significance: 5 per cent

The data analysis presented in the above table indicates that there exist differences in the mean score of consumers' agreeability on the benefits of green products and their buying intentions based on their family type.

Table 4.61: Result of Anova Consumers' Level of Agreeability about Benefits Obtained by Buying Green Products Vs their Family Income

Variables	Source	Sum of Square	DF	Mean Square	F	Sig
Green products ensure healthy lifestyle	Between Groups	.446	1	.446	1.627	.203
	Within Groups	205.133	748	.274		
	Total	205.579	749	-		
Green products help to maintain a healthy home and family	Between Groups	1.017	1	1.017	3.981	.046
	Within Groups	190.983	748	.255		
	Total	192.000	749	-		
Green products prevent us from using harmful chemicals	Between Groups	9.728	1	9.728	21.463	.000
	Within Groups	339.046	748	.453		
	Total	348.775	749	-		
Green products are risk free products (both on human and on environment)	Between Groups	4.339	1	4.339	10.549	.001
	Within Groups	307.636	748	.411		
	Total	311.975	749	-		
Green products are price-wise reasonable	Between Groups	18.397	1	18.397	27.273	.000
	Within Groups	504.570	748	.675		

Variables	Source	Sum of Square	DF	Mean Square	F	Sig
	Total	522.967	749	-		
Green products are reusable	Between Groups	24.430	1	24.430	41.740	.000
	Within Groups	437.785	748	.585		
	Total	462.215	749	-		
Green products ensure energy efficiency and save scarce resources	Between Groups	51.718	1	51.718	70.687	.000
	Within Groups	547.274	748	.732		
	Total	598.992	749	-		
Green products ensure sustainability of modern earth	Between Groups	22.142	1	22.142	33.527	.000
	Within Groups	493.997	748	.660		
	Total	516.139	749	-		
Green products gives us freedom from the guilty feeling of harming environment	Between Groups	35.953	1	35.953	59.264	.000
	Within Groups	453.782	748	.607		
	Total	489.735	749	-		
Now-a-days there are innumerable, products in the market in the name of green products	Between Groups	17.453	1	17.453	25.008	.000
	Within Groups	522.045	748	.698		
	Total	539.499	749	-		

Level of Significance: 5 per cent

From the above table it has been inferred that probability value of ANOVA at 5 per cent level does establish a good relationship between the variables tested. Therefore, the hypothesis framed stands accepted and it has been concluded that consumers' level of agreeability about benefits obtained by buying green products differ based on their family income level. However, it has been found that family health is not always compromised on the income level. From the elaborate data discussion made in the tables: 4.32 -4.49, it has been inferred that consumers' level of agreeability about benefits obtained by buying green products varies among their demographic and socio–economic status. Thus, the hypothesis framed stands accepted. The empirical findings made by Sharma and Trivedi (2016) were found on be on a par with the conclusion drawn in this section of the study. Sharma and Trivedi (2016) study had stated that demographics status of consumers have directly affected green consumers' buying behaviour. The study found that each variable is equally significant for the green marketer. The study findings also reveal that there are enough evidences available and it clearly states that all the green marketing variables affect consumers in a positive way towards the purchase of green products and the marketers should take a keen note of them in order to get the best marketing strategy. Factor analysis is often used in data reduction to identify a small number of factors that explain most of the variance observed in a much larger number of manifest variables. In the current study rotation factor analysis is performed to measure the consumers' level of agreeability about benefits obtained by buying green products. Explorative Factor analysis technique has been applied to find the underlying dimension (factors) that exists among 10 variables relating to the consumers' level of agreeability about benefits obtained from buying green products.

Table 4.62: KMO and Bartlett's Test Consumers' Level of Agreeability about Benefits Obtained by Buying Green Products

Kaiser-Meyer-Olkin Measure of Sampling Adequacy	.690
Bartlett's Test of Sphericity Approx. Chi-Square	2243.535
DF	45
Sig	.000

Level of Significance: 5 per cent

In the present study, Kaiser-Meyer-Olkin (KMO) Measure of Sampling Adequacy (MSA) and Bartlett's test of Sphericity were applied to verify the adequacy or appropriateness of data for factor analysis. In this study, the value of KMO for overall matrix was found to be excellent (.690) and Bartlett's test of Sphericity was highly significant (p<0.05). Bartlett's Sphericity test was effective, as the chi-square value draws significance at five per cent level. The results thus indicated that the sample taken was appropriate to proceed with a factor analysis procedure. Besides Bartlett's Test of Sphericity and KMO Measure of sampling Adequacy, Communality values of all variables were also observed.

Table 4.63: Cumulative Consumers' Level of Agreeability about Benefits Obtained by Buying Green Products

Factors	Initial	Extraction
Green products ensure healthy lifestyle	1.000	.846
Green products help to maintain a healthy home and family	1.000	.688
Green products prevent us from using harmful chemicals	1.000	.775
Green products are risk free products (both on human and on environment)	1.000	.790
Green products are price-wise reasonable	1.000	.618
Green products are reusable	1.000	.818
Green products ensure energy efficiency and save scarce resources	1.000	.822
Green products ensure sustainability of modern earth	1.000	.806
Green products gives us freedom from the guilty feeling of harming environment	1.000	.788
Now-a-days there are innumerable, products in the market in the name of green products	1.000	.816

Level of Significance: 5 per cent

In order to provide a more parsimonious interpretation of the results, 10-item scale was then factor-analyzed using the Principal Component method with Varimax rotation. Factor analysis attempts to identify the underlying variables, or factors, that explain the pattern of correlations within a set of observed variables. The significance of relationship between the variables is depicted in the following table.

Table 4.64: Rotated Component Matrix Consumers' Level of Agreeability about Benefits Obtained by Buying Green Products

Factors	Factors				
	F_1	F_2	F_3	F_4	F_5
X_1 - Green products ensure healthy lifestyle	-	-	.899	-	-
X_2 - Green products help to maintain a healthy home and family	-	-	.726	-	-
X_3 - Green products prevent us from using harmful chemicals	-	.712	-	-	-
X_4 - Green products are risk free products (both on human and on environment)	-	-	-	.793	-
X_5 - Green products are price-wise reasonable	.523	-	-	-	.502
X_6 - Green products are reusable	.846	--	-	-	-
X_7 - Green products ensure energy efficiency and save scarce resources	.809	-	-	-	-
X_8 - Green products ensure sustainability of modern earth	-	-	-	.822	-
X_9 - Green products gives us freedom from the guilty feeling of harming environment	-	.811	-	-	-
X_{10} - Now-a-days there are innumerable, products in the market in the name of green products	-	-	-	-	.847
Eigen value	1.993	1.569	1.546	1.464	1.254
% of Variance	19.326	15.692	15.460	14.643	12.539
Cumulative%	19.326	35.018	50.479	65.121	77.990

Level of Significance: 5 per cent

Through an analysis of items in each factor, new dimensions were defined (Table 4.64), excluding items with a value lower than 0.5. Five factors extracted together account for 77.990 per cent of the total variance (information contained in the original 10 variables). This is pretty good, because the researcher is able to economize on the number of variables (from 10 the researcher has reduced them to five underlying factors), while the data lost only about 22.01 per cent of the information content (77.990 per cent is retained by the five factors extracted out of the 10 original variables). Since the idea of factor analysis is to identify the factors that meaningfully summarize the sets of closely related variables, the rotation phase of the factor analysis attempts to transfer initial matrix into one that is easier to interpret. Varimax rotation method is used to extract meaningful factors.

Five factors were identified as being maximum percentage variance accounted. The variables X_5, X_6 and X_7 are grouped as factor I and it accounts for 19.326 per cent of the total variance. The variables X_3 and X_9 constitute the factor II and it accounts for 15.692 per cent of the total variance. The variables X_1 and X_2 are grouped as factor III and it accounts for 15.460 per cent of the total variance. The variables X_4 and X_8 are grouped as factor IV and it accounts for 14.643 per cent of the total variance. The variables X_5 and X_{10} constitute the factor V and it accounts for 12.539 per cent of the total variance.

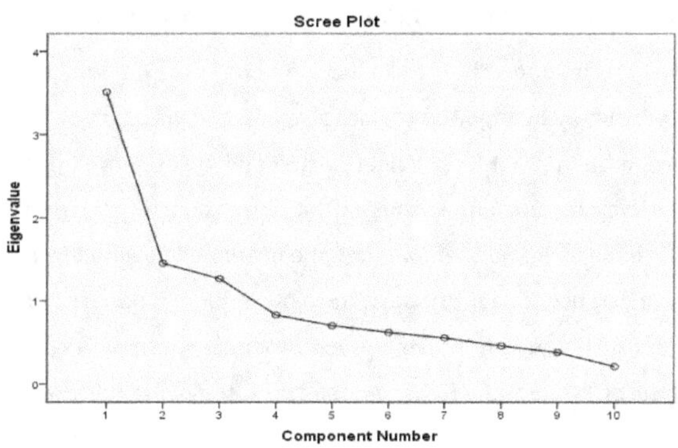

Exhibit 4.12: Scree Plot Consumers' Level of Agreeability about Benefits Obtained by Buying Green Products

A Scree plot is a graph that plots the total variance associated with each factor. It is a visual display of how many factors there are in the data. The Scree plot graphs the Eigenvalue against the factor number. It has been observed that although there are 10 principal components only 3 factors have Eigenvalues over one. So it can expect three principal components in the data. The curve indicates the inflexion on the curve.

Table 4.65: Summary of Rotation Factor Analysis & Cronbach's Alpha Consumers' Level of Agreeability about Benefits Obtained by Buying Green Products

Factors	Variables Included in the Factors	Cronbach's Alpha
F_1	Green products are price-wise reasonable, Green products are reusable and Green products ensure energy efficiency and save scarce resources	.869
F_2	Green products prevent us from using harmful chemicals and Green products gives us freedom from the guilty feeling of harming environment	.780
F_3	Green products ensure healthy lifestyle and Green products help to maintain a healthy home and family	.676
F_4	Green products are risk free products (both on human and on environment) and Green products ensure sustainability of modern earth	.635
F_5	Green products are price-wise reasonable and Now-a-days there are innumerable, products in the market in the name of green products	.600

Source: Computed From Primary Data

The internal consistency of each factor was estimated individually using the alpha coefficient of Cronbach's (α). Factor analysis was applied to establish and reveal the correlation between consumers' level of agreeability about benefits obtained by buying green products. The Cronbach's reliability values of.869, .780, .676, .635, and .600 indicate a significant correlation between the variables tested and a good internal consistency.

4.1.7. *Problems Faced by the Consumers' of Green Products*

Marketers have the responsibility to make the consumers understand the need for and benefits of green products as compared to non-green ones. This step will help the marketers to sustain themselves in the market for a longer period and at the same time it will help them in understanding the factors that either motivate or limit consumers from not consuming of green products. To have a clear understanding of consumers' psychology about the markets it is of paramount importance to identify the nature of problems that are currently encountered by green consumers while buying or using green products. To draw a clear understanding on this concept analysis of Tables: 4.66 to 67 and interpretation were performed.

Table 4.66: Nature of Problems Faced While Buying or Consuming of Green Products

Si.No	Problem	No.of respondents	Percentage
1.	Faced Problems	384	51.20
2.	Did Not Face Problems	366	48.80
	Total	750	100

Source: Primary Data

From the above table it has been inferred that majority (51.20per cent) of the respondents have said that they have faced problems while buying green products and the remaining of 48.80per cent of the respondents did not face any problems while buying green products.

Hence, it has been concluded that majority (51.20per cent) of the respondents have said that they have faced problems while buying green products. It has been understood that there exist differences in the idealism about the green products and its reality in practical practices.

Table 4.66(A): Nature of Problems Faced While Buying or Consuming of Green Products

Problems	Sum	Mean	Rank
High Cost	1106	2.87	10
Improper product Availability	1475	3.82	9
Fraudulent Behaviour in Manufacturing / Marketing	1945	5.04	8
Fake Certification	1969	5.10	7
Unable to differentiate between conventional and non-conventional products	2190	5.67	6
Inadequate Labelling	2281	5.91	4
Limited availability of the products	2259	5.85	5
Insufficient Government / NGO, etc support to enhance product knowledge	2688	6.96	2
Limited Scientific Certification	2623	6.80	3
Others	2800	7.25	1

Source: Primary Data

The above table discusses the nature of problems faced while buying or consuming of green products. Majority of consumers fear buying green products due to various reasons like: fear of malpractices, lack of trust, past bad experiences etc. These reasons are ranked in first place with the mean score of 7.25. Most of the respondents claim dissatisfaction with insufficient government/NGO support to enhance product knowledge, limited scientific certification, inadequate labelling, limited availability of the products etc., these reasons of limitations are ranked in second, third, fourth and fifth places with the mean score of 6.96, 6.80, 5.91 and 5.85 respectively. Similarly, respondents' claims that they are unable to differentiate between conventional and non-conventional products, moreover fear of fake certification, fraudulent behaviour in manufacturing/marketing, improper product availability in the retail outlets and high cost of green products are considered as frequently faced issues related with green product consumptions. These factors are ranked in sixth, seventh, eighth, ninth and tenth places with the mean score of 5.67, 5.10, 5.04, 3.82 and 2.87 correspondingly.

Thus it has been concluded that majority (72.50 per cent) (mean score 7.25) of the consumers fear buying green products due to various reasons like: fear of malpractices, lack of trust, past bad experiences etc.

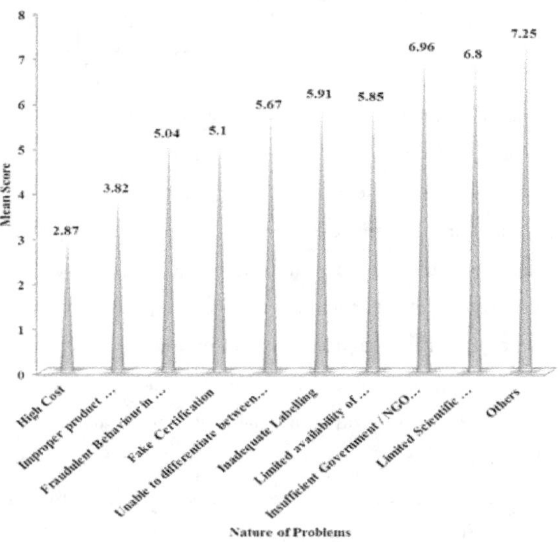

Exhibit 4.13: Nature of Problems Faced While Buying Or Consuming of Green Products

Modern day marketers of green products face greatest challenges like: changes in consumer preferences for the green products, suspicion of eco-friendly advertising claim, unfavourable consumer perception of green products, high product cost and the high cost invested in developing green products. These challenges are faced by the marketers because of the concern for the environmental problems that are high among the consumers. Drawing relevance from the above discussion the following hypothesis is framed and tested.

H8: It is generally believed that an green product consumer faces fewer problems.

Table 4.67: Independent Z-Testproblems Faced by Consumers' While Buying Green Products

| Particulars | Green Products | | | | Z | DF | Sig |
| | Faced Problems | | Did Not Faced Problems | | | | |
	Mean	SD	Mean	SD			
High Cost	2.83	3.456	10.00	.000	-2.931	384	.004
Improper product Availability	3.79	1.900	9.00	.000	-3.870	384	.000
Fraudulent Behaviour in Manufacturing/Marketing	8.00	.000	5.02	3.057	-1.375	384	.170
Fake Certification	7.00	.000	5.09	3.046	-.885	384	.377
Unable to differentiate between conventional and non-conventional products	4.00	.000	5.68	2.273	1.045	384	.297
Inadequate Labelling	5.00	.000	5.91	1.638	.788	384	.431
Limited availability of the products	6.00	.000	5.85	2.556	-.082	384	.935
Insufficient Government/NGO, etc. support to enhance product knowledge	1.00	.000	6.99	2.538	3.335	384	.001
Scientific Certification	2.00	.000	6.82	2.451	2.778	384	.006
Others	3.00	.000	7.28	2.641	2.287	384	.023

Level of Significance: 5 per cent

From the above table it has been inferred that the probability value of Z is not found to be significant at five per cent level in certain cases and probability value of Z is found to be significant at five per cent level in few other cases. Therefore the hypothesis framed stands partially accepted and partially rejected. Eco-friendly i.e., green product consumers face certain problems like: fraudulent behaviour in manufacturing/marketing, fake certification, consumers unable to differentiate between conventional and non-conventional products, inadequate labelling and limited availability of the products. On the other hand it has been observed that consumers do not mind paying extra money for the consumption of green products, they like to wait for the product availability in the market and exhibit trust on the Government certification and scientific certification and other related information passed in this issue. The study finding is complemented with the empirical findings and conclusion made by Terenggana et al. (2013), Nagaraju B. and Thejaswini H. (2014) and Sachdev (2011). Terenggana et al. (2013) found that the variable consumers' trust is an important factor and a central point to find which variables significantly influence attitudes, risk perception, perceived quality and consumer purchase intent. Nagaraju B. and Thejaswini H. (2014) found that majority of the consumers feel that price of the eco-friendly FMCG products is higher when it is compared with non-eco-friendly FMCG products. The study suggests that the government, the organization and the customers have to put hands together in creating awareness about green products. Sachdev (2011) concluded by stating that the paramount significance is going to be attached to eco-friendly products as they shall come to occupy the center stage in the coming years. Commensurate with that, there will be a shift in consumers' perception albeit at a low pace in the coming years.

Lim et al. (2013) argue that consumers have a lack of understanding of what is meant by green products as consumers only evaluated a product to be green based on the final product itself without evaluating production and manufacturing processes. Because of such limited understanding, consumers are not able to see the potentially fruitful impact of purchasing and consuming green products towards environmental sustainability. Further, the misconception of green products with recyclable products poses a threat to authentic green products. In particular, authentic green products have to be environmentally friendly from its inception in the production and manufacturing process right until the disposal of the products, which could either be bio-degradable or recyclable, and not just limited to recyclability. There is also existence of ignorance in consumers' minds. More specifically, consumers were found to be ignorant as: (i) they believe efforts, such as purchasing and consuming green products, from one person will have no significant effect on the environment; (ii) personal well-being is more important and environmental well-being is less important, in which environmental well-being becomes important only when it affects consumers' personal well-being; and (iii) efforts to save the environment should be left to environmentalists. Such ignorance is translated into a 'not-bothering' attitude towards green products.

This contributes to a lack of demand and non-existence of favourable perceptions and attitudes toward green products.

4.1.8. Consumers' Intention Towards Future Buying of Green Products

The failure or success in any business is dependable upon the behaviour of the end-user or consumer who finally uses the product or any services.

This behaviour of the consumer greatly impacts their decision to purchase or not purchase the product. Depending on their decision and their usage, an organization decides which products to manufacture and to continue. The positioning of the product is dependent on the consumption of the product and this behaviour of consumers may be related to any kind of products or services. This discussion emphasizes the importance of consumers' decision on the marketers and manufacturers survival. To draw an introspective view of the sample consumers on their future buying behaviour the analysis of the following Tables: 4.68 to 4.73 and discussions are performed.

Table 4.68: Consumers' Opinion on Continuing to Buy Green Products

Sl. No	Opinion	No. of Respondents	Percentage
1.	Very Surely	202	26.93
2.	Surely	456	60.80
3.	Seldom	46	6.13
4.	Not Sure	45	6.00
5.	Never Buy	1	0.13
	Total	750	100

Source: Primary Data

From the above presented data it has been inferred that 60.80 per cent of the respondents have said that they surely prefer buying green products in future. 26.93 per cent of the respondents have said that they believe that they will very surely buy green products in future too and 6.13 per cent of the respondents are not so sure about their buying decisions and the remaining 6 per cent of the respondents are not sure about their future buying behaviour. Whereas, 0.13 per cent of the respondents have claimed that they will never prefer buying green products in the near future.

It has been concluded that 60.80 per cent of the respondents have said that they surely prefer buying green product in future. This is purely due to the rapid increase for the environment concern in the last two decades.

Marketing literature suggests that there is a relationship between customer satisfaction and loyalty. Satisfaction leads to attitudinal loyalty. It could be seen as the intension to purchase. Based on this concept the following hypothesis is framed and tested.

H9: Consumers' level of satisfaction towards green products influences their preference of continuing to buy green products in future.

The multiple regression analysis was performed to evaluate the Consumers' level of satisfaction towards green products and its influence over their preference of continuing to buy green products in future.

The dependent variable considered was consumers' that influences their preference of continuing to buy green products in future and the independent variables : X_1 = Availability of green products in the market, X_2= Genuineness of the product (Reliability, X_3= Easy accessibility to green products, X_4= Creative, innovative and modernisation Features incorporated in the product (s), X_5= Price of the products X_6= Quality of the products, X_7= Promotion of the products, X_8= Offers & discounts, X_9= Product varieties available, X_{10}= Durability of the product (long–lasting) and X_{11}= insurances for Eco-friendly features like labelling.

Consumers' level of satisfaction towards green products = f (Availability of green products in the market, Genuineness of the product (Reliability), Easy accessibility to green products, Creative, innovative and modernisation features incorporated in the product, Price of the products, Quality of the products, promotion of the products, offers & discounts, product varieties available, Durability of the product (long-lasting) and insurances for Eco-friendly features like labelling.

Measured Consumers' level of satisfaction towards green products was considered as dummy variable and run the following regression model to identify the consumers' level of satisfaction towards green products influences their preference of continuing to buy green products in future.

Consumers' level of satisfaction towards green products influences their preference of continuing to buy green products in future.

$$(Y1) = \beta 0 + \beta 1 X1 + \beta 2 X2 + \beta 3 X3 + \beta 4 X4 + \beta 5 X5 + \beta 6 X6 + \beta 7 X7 + \beta 8 X8 + \beta 9 X9 + \beta 10 X10 + \beta 11 X11 + e$$

Where,

Y1= Consumers' level of satisfaction towards green products

$\beta 0$ = Intercept

$\beta 1$-$\beta 11$= Slopes (estimates of coefficients

X_1= Availability of green products in the market

X_2= Genuineness of the Product (Reliability)

X_3= Easy accessibility to green products

X_4= Creative, Innovative and Modernisation Features Incorporated in the Products

X_5= Price of the products

X_6= Quality of the Products,

X_7= Promotion of the Products

X_8= Offers & Discounts

X_9= Product Varieties Available

X_{10}= Durability of the Product (long-lasting)

X_{11}= Insurances for Eco-friendly Features like Labelling and

e = Random error, which the researcher assumed as NID for this research.

Table 4.69: Multiple Regression Model Summaryconsumers' Level of Satisfaction towards Green Products Influences their Preference of Continuing to Buy Green Products in Future

R	R²	Adjusted R²	SE	F Value	Sig
.568	.322	.312	.659	19.675	.000

Level of Significance: 5 per cent

$$Y = 1.234 + .146X_1 + .045X_2 + .143X_3.311X_4 + .019X_5 + .006X_6 + .139X_7 + .132X_8$$

$$311X_9 + .618X_{10} - 212X_{11}$$

It has been revealed from the above econometric analysis that F ratio (19.675) is statistically significant at 5 per cent level. This indicates that the entire regression is significant, and it establishes 56.80 per cent of the relationship between the variables tested. From the above table it is seen that the coefficient of correlation (R) value .568 describes a good relationship between variables and the coefficient of determinant (R^2) .322 value establishes a significant association between the 11 variables tested. Therefore the hypothesis framed stands accepted and it has been concluded that Consumers' level of satisfaction towards green products influences their preference of continuing to buy green products in future. The following table shows the value of constant and coefficient value of each attributes to analyse the Consumers' level of satisfaction towards green products and its influence over their preference of continuing to buy green products in future.

Table 4.70: Consumers' Level of Satisfaction towards Green Products Influences their Preference of Continuing to Buy Green Products in Future

Variables	Unstandardized Coefficients		Standardized Coefficients	t	Sig.
	B	Std. Error	Beta		
Constant	1.234	.123	-	10.022	.000
Availability of green products in the market	.146	.051	.122	2.877	.004
Genuineness of the Product (Reliability)	.045	.053	.036	.850	.396
Easy accessibility to green products	.143	.049	.125	2.926	.004
Creative, Innovative and Modernisation Features Incorporated in the Products	-.311	.054	-.236	-5.782	.000
Price of the products	.019	.044	.020	.425	.671
Quality of the Products	.006	.039	.006	.152	.879
Promotion of the Products	.139	.037	.149	3.765	.000
Offers & Discounts	.132	.041	.129	3.195	.001
Product Varieties Available	-.311	.043	-.333	-7.264	.000
Durability of the Product (long-lasting)	.618	.055	.612	11.298	.000
Insurances for Eco-friendly Features like labelling	-.212	.045	-.244	-4.741	.000

Level of Significance: 5 per cent

To determine of one or more of the independent variables are significant with the predictors and to analyse whether consumers' level of satisfaction towards green products influences their preference of continuing to buy green products in future, with the information provided above the co-efficient table is examined.

Out of eleven parameters statements considered only eight were statistically significant. The standardized co-efficient beta column reveals that consumer level of satisfaction towards green products have met beta standard co-efficient 1.234 which is statistically significant at 0.000.

Predicated Value of

Consumer level of satisfaction towards green products

= +1.234 (Constant)

+.146 (Availability of green products in the market)

+.143 (Easy accessibility to green products)

±.311 (Creative, Innovative and Modernisation Features Incorporated in the Product)

+.139 (Promotion of the Products)

+.132 (Offers & Discounts)

±.311 (Product Varieties Available)

+.618(Durability of the Product (long-lasting)

±.212 (Insurances for Eco-friendly Features like labelling).

To assess whether the Consumers' level of satisfaction towards green products, the multiple regression modeling was performed and to the relative importance of the individual dimension of the generated scale, Multiple Regression Analysis indicated that out of eleven variables tested eight variables: Availability of green products in the market , Easy accessibility to green products, Creative, innovative and modernization features incorporated in the product ,Promotion of the products, Offers & discounts, product varieties available, Durability of the product (long-lasting), Insurances for Eco-friendly features like labelling ,were found to be statistically significant. The empirical findings made by Singh et al. (2014) is found to be in accord with the conclusion made in this section of the study. Singh et al. (2014) study findings indicate that consumers who are already buying green products and those who are satisfied by the previous purchases are willing to repeat purchases.

Table 4.71: Consumers' Opinion on Usage of Green Products Against Non- Conventional Materials

Sl. No	Usage	No. of respondents	Percentage
1.	Using	446	59.47
2.	Not-using	304	40.53
	Total	750	100

Source: Primary Data

From the above table it has been inferred that 59.47 per cent of the respondents have been using green products and the remaining 40.53 per cent of the respondents do not use green products since they prefer using non-conventional products.

Hence, 59.47 per cent of the respondents have been using green products instead of non-conventional products.

Table 4.72: Reasons Stated by Consumers' For Usage of Green Products Against Conventional Materials

Sl. No	Reasons	No. of Respondents (N=1980)	Proportionate Percentage
1.	Growing Awareness about green products among consumers	408	91.48
2.	Growing concern of manufacturers towards environment protection	338	75.78
3.	Awareness Created by Social Bodies	377	84.53
4.	Awareness created by the Government	420	94.17
5.	Changing Peoples' Attitude towards Usage of Traditional Products	437	97.98

Source: Primary Data

From the above table it has been inferred that on an average of 97.98 per cent of the respondents prefer using green products due to change in their attitude towards usage of traditional products. 94.17 per cent of the respondents have said that they prefer green products influenced by the awareness created by the government agencies. Similarly 91.48 per cent of the respondents have said that consuming green products and bodies have increased in recent years due to growing awareness about green products among consumers. 84.53 per cent of the respondents have said that they prefer green products after the awareness created by social bodies. Further, 75.78 per cent of the respondents have also opined that usage of green products have increased in recent years as manufacturers of various consumers goods have started focusing more on environment protection, so they have stated to introduce more traditional products in an innovative concept like introduction of eco-friendly brown sugar, plum sugar (powdered format), herbal products etc.

Hence it has been concluded that, majority i.e., on an average of 97.98 per cent of the respondents prefer using green products for the following reasons: Changing people's attitude towards usage of traditional products.

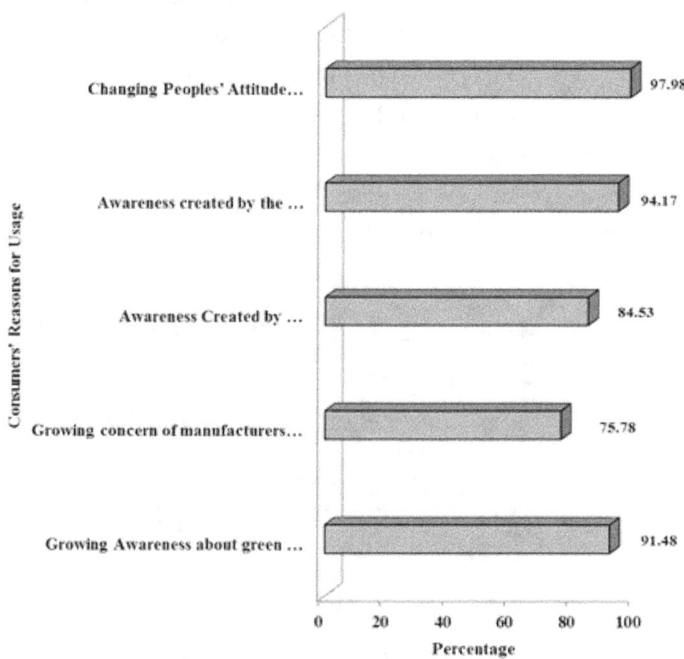

Exhibit 4.14: Reasons Stated by Consumers for Usage of Green Products Against Conventional Materials

Table 4.73: Reasons Stated by the Consumers for Not Using Green Products

S.No	Reasons	No. of Respondents (N=1293)	Proportionate Percentage
1.	High Cost of the Products	299	98.36
2.	Lack of Genuineness of Products Available in the Market	241	79.28
3.	Poor Promotions and Offers	206	67.76
4.	Lack of Awareness among Consumers	247	81.25
5.	Less Initiatives taken by Government of Environment Protection	300	98.68

Source: Primary Data

The detailed data analysis indicates that 40 per cent of consumers feel that Government of India has not actively promoted eco-friendly i.e., green products, and so this act has restricted them from actively consuming green products. 98.36 per cent of the respondents have said that they do not prefer green products as cost of the products are very high. Similarly 81.25 per cent of the respondents consuming has revealed that most of modern day consumers lack awareness about green products that in turn restrict them from consuming these products. 79.28 per cent of the respondents have said that many consumers fear about the genuineness of products available in the market and that could be one of the reasons for low consumption of the products. 67.76 per cent of the respondents have also opined that Poor Promotions & Offers are also one among the reasons for poor consumption of these products.

Hence it has been concluded that, majority i.e., on an average of 98.68per cent of respondents' are not using green products as these products not well promoted by Government of India.

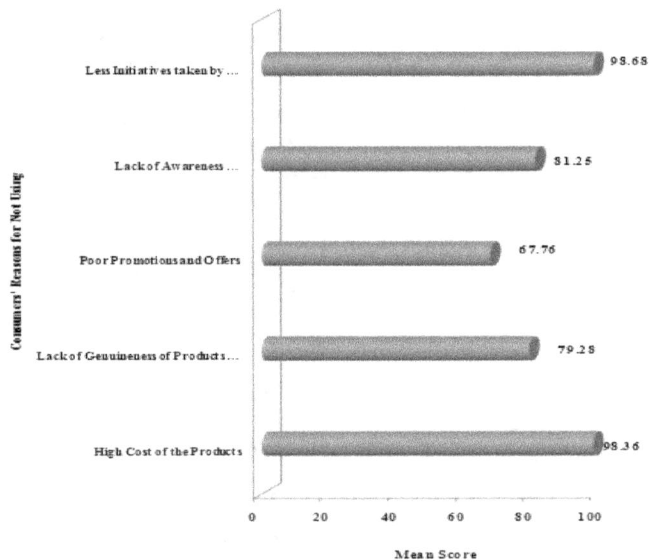

Exhibit 4.15: Reasons Stated by the Consumers for Noting using Green Product

4.1.9. *Structural Equation Model*

Consumers are becoming more and more aware of environmental issues and this has increased the demand for ecological products. If consumers have a favourable attitude toward greening environment, they are more inclined to purchase green products. The continuous awareness of environmental problems may in turn change consumers' attitudes and purchase intentions as well. Further, it has been observed that environmental concerns play an important role on consumers' intention to purchase green products. Thus, environmental concerns are not the only factor for the consumers to purchase environmentally friendly products. There are other factors that lead to the purchases. Similarly, it can be claimed that consumers' perceptions have a positive effect on their purchase intention of green or say eco-friendly products. Furthermore, for consumers who often indulge in purchasing organic brands products believe that the ownership of organic products not only gives them personal satisfaction but also makes them feel accepted and recognized by like-minded people or the people of the same group. The discussion made above provides reasonable support for framing Structural Equation Model and for framing the hypothesised relationships between the variables.

Table 4.74: Variables Expansion

Awareness	Consumers' awareness towards green products
AttEco	Consumers' level of attitude towards Eco-friendliness
AttiProd	Consumers' level of attitude towards green products
Factors	Factors that influence buying green products
Products	Consumers' buying behaviour of green products
Perception	Consumers' level of perception towards green products
Satisfaction	Consumers' level of satisfaction towards green products

Table 4.75: Testing of Hypotheses Results Association Between Consumer Awareness, Attitude, Product Purchased Perception and Satisfaction towards Green Products

Sl.No	Statement (H_0)	Remark
H10	There exists a close association between consumers' attitude towards eco-friendliness and their awareness towards green products.	Positive Confirmed
H11	There exists a close association between attitude exhibited by the consumers while purchasing of green products and their awareness towards its	Positive Confirmed
H12	There exists a close association between consumers' awareness towards green products and factors that motivated them to buy the green products.	Negative Not Confirmed
H13	There exists a close association between factors that motivated consumers to buy the green products and the nature of products bought by them.	Positive Confirmed
H14	There exists a close association between consumers' attitude towards eco-friendliness and the nature of products bought by them.	Positive Confirmed
H15	There exists a close association between consumers' attitude towards green products and the nature of products bought by them	Positive Confirmed
H16	There exists a close association between consumers' perception towards green product and the nature of products bought by them	Negative Not Confirmed
H17	There exists a close association between consumers' satisfaction towards green product sand the nature of products bought by them	Positive Confirmed

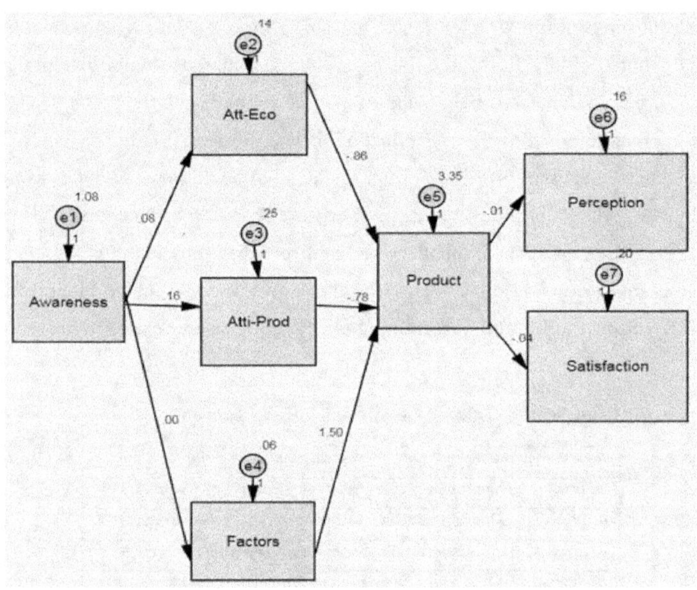

Exhibit 4.16: Structural Equation Modelling Analysis Goodness of Fit Model

Table 4.76: Chi-Square Result and Goodness of Fit Indices of the Proposed Model

Fit Indices	Obtained Value	Accepted Thresholds Levels	Acceptable Value
$\chi 2$ Chi-square	376.934	NA	NA
Scaled $\chi 2/df$	13/0.000	<0.05	<0.05
Goodness of Fit Index (GFI)	.877	Value Greater than 0.95	0-1
Adjusted Goodness of Fit Index(AGFI)	.736	Value Greater than 0.95	0-1
Tucker-Lewis Index (TLI)	.002	Value Greater than 0.95	0-1
Comparative Fit Index (CFI)	.382	Value Greater than 0.95	0-1
Normed Fit Index (NFI)	.382	Value Greater than 0.95	0-1
Parsimonious Normed Fit Index (PNFI)	.237	0=Poor Fit, 1=Good Fit	0-1
Parsimonious Comparative Fit Index (PCFI)	.237	0=Poor Fit, 1=Good Fit	0-1
Relative Fit Index (RFI)	.002	0=Poor Fit, 1=Good Fit	0-1
Incremental Fit Index (IFI)	.390	0=Poor Fit, 1=Good Fit	0-1
Root Mean Square Approximation Method (RMSEA)	.000	Value less than 0.07	.05 or less would indicate a close fit of the model

Level of Significance: 5 per cent

On the basis of these measurements, the result of the study shows that the proposed model has a reasonable data fit χ^2=376.934 (p=.000), GFI=.877, AGFI-.736, TLI=.002, CFI=.382, NFI=.382, PNFI=.237, PCFI=.237, RFI=-.002, IFI=.390, RMSEA=.000).

Table 4.77: Path Analysis Structure Maximum Likelihood –Regression Weightage

Path			Unstandardized Estimates (β)	S.E	C.R	P Value	Relationship
AttEco	<---	Awareness	.075	.013	5.788	.000	Significant
AttiProd	<---	Awareness	.160	.018	9.070	.000	Significant
Factors	<---	Awareness	-.005	.008	-.549	.583	Insignificant
Product	<---	Factors	1.501	.283	5.298	.000	Significant
Product	<---	AttiProd	-.777	.127	-6.131	.000	Significant
Product	<---	AttEco	-.864	.177	-4.876	.000	Significant
Perception	<---	Product	-.013	.008	-1.734	.083	Insignificant
Satisfaction	<---	Product	-.042	.008	-5.041	.000	Significant

The study observed that the measure of co-efficient of variances reveals that consumers' attitude towards eco-friendliness, green products, awareness and their satisfaction are found to be significant: attitude towards eco-friendliness vs. awareness (β=0.075, p=.000), attitude towards green product vs. awareness (β=.160, p=.000), product vs. factors (β=1.501, p=.000), product vs. attitude towards green products (β=.777, p=.000), product vs. attitude towards eco-friendliness (β=.864, p=.000) and satisfaction vs. green products (β=.042, p=.000). The measures of co-efficient of variances are negatively correlated and to be statistically insignificant with factors vs. awareness (β=.005, p=.583) and perception vs. product (β=.013, p=.083). The study concluded by stating that out of eight hypotheses framed six hypotheses were found to be accepted and two were rejected.

The study results confirm that there exists a close association between consumers' awareness towards green products vs. their attitude towards eco-friendliness and the attitude exhibited by them while purchasing green products. The study also found that there exists a close association between consumers' attitude, factors that motivated consumers to buy the green products and their satisfaction vs. the product bought by them. The study observed that there exists a negative association between consumers' awareness towards green products and factors that motivated them to buy the green products. Similarly, there exist no association between consumers' perception towards green product and the products bought by them.

4.2. Conclusion

As per the survey results 54.93 per cent of the respondents are females and 45.07 per cent of the respondents are males. The study observed that 29.07 per cent of the respondents are in the age group of 25-30 years and 30.80 per cent of the respondents have completed UG degree. The study found that 36 per cent of the respondents have moderate level of awareness towards green products. In association with the consumers' awareness, it has been observed that 40.80 per cent of the respondents always prefer buying green products. The study indicated that 97.73 per cent of the respondents have sourced information about green products from yoga class, art of living class, seminars, public gathering and from other naturopathy classes etc. In relevance to this finding the study indicated that 77.73 per cent of the respondents have said that they identified the green products through the nature ingredients used in manufacturing of the products, so majority of consumers believe that green products are better than non-conventional products. Similarly, the study also found that majority (79.40per cent) (mean score of 3.97) of the consumers pay attention to the advertisement claim made about the products and try to frame an attitude towards the products and 36.40 per cent of the respondents have said that the friends and colleagues mostly influence their perception towards green products and their values. The study noticed that 58.93 per cent of the respondents have been consuming green products for the past 1-3 years. Majority of consumers have said long usage of organic products in the family greatly influenced their adoption towards modern day innovative green products. In Support, to the above statement majority of respondents' believe that green products are healthier and safer. It has been observed that 81.80 per cent of consumers have exhibited high degree of satisfaction towards the green products available in the market. As per the survey results, majority of the consumers have benefited from having a healthy home and family and conversion to healthy life-styles, due to consumption of green products. The study indicated that 51.20 per cent of the respondents have said that they have faced problems while buying green products and majority of consumers' fear of buying green products is due to various reasons like: fear of malpractices, lack of trust, past bad experiences etc. Out of 750 respondents surveyed 60.80 per cent of the respondents have said that they surely prefer buying green products in future.

Results of statistical analysis revealed that there is an association between consumers' awareness towards green products and their demographic and socio-economic status. Moreover, consumers' level of awareness towards green products helps in recognising a product as eco-friendly or not. Similarly, consumers' level of awareness towards green products influences their level of attitude towards it. The empirical results indicated that factors that influence consumers to buy green products differ from one individual to another. Consumers' level of attitude towards green products influences their level of perceptions towards it. The study confirmed that there exists a close association between consumers' level of perception towards green products and level of satisfaction towards it. The study inferred that consumers' level of agreeability about benefits obtained by buying green products varies among their demographic and socio–economic status. The study findings mentioned thateco-friendly i.e., green product consumers face certain problems like: fraudulent behaviour in manufacturing/marketing, fake certification, consumers are unable to differentiate between conventional and non-conventional products, inadequate labeling and limited availability of the products. On the other hand, it has been observed that consumers do not mind paying extra money for the consumption of green products, and they like to wait for the product availability in the market and exhibit trust on the Government certification and scientific certification and other related information passed in this issue. Consumers' level of satisfaction towards green products influences their preference of continuing to buy green products in future. The study results also confirmed that there exists a close association between consumers' awareness towards green products and their attitude towards eco-friendliness and the attitude exhibited by them while purchasing green products. The study also found that there exists a close association between consumers' attitude, factors that motivated consumers to buy green products and their satisfaction towards the products bought by them. The study observed that there exists a negative association between consumers' awareness towards green products and factors that motivated them to buy the green products. Similarly, there exists no association between consumers' perception towards green products and the products bought by them.

Chapter V

Summary, Findings, Suggestions, Conclusion and Scope for Further Research

The final and fifth chapter of this elaborate empirical study aims to present a brief summary of the statement of the problem, the purpose of the study and the methodology used in the investigation, the findings, the suggestions proposed by the researcher and conclusion.

5.1.   Summary of the Study

Green marketing is a phenomenon which has developed particular importance in the modern market. It has emerged as an important concept in India as in other parts of the developing and developed countries. The consumers play a major role in determining the demand for any product and since green products are eco-friendly, they have created a niche for those environmental consciousness customers. This study aims to analyse consumers' attitude, preferences and buying practices towards green products. This study is focused on the green consumers living in Coimbatore City of Tamil Nadu. The following objectives are framed for effective conduct of this study. The first objective of the study aimed to study the demographic and socio-economic status of green product consumers living in Coimbatore city. The second and third objectives focused to analyse the consumers' awareness and attitude towards green products available in the market and to critically evaluate the green–products buying behaviour among consumers. The fourth and fifth objectives of the study tend to measure the consumers' perception and satisfaction towards green products available in the market and to measure the prevailing gap in the consumers' perception and satisfaction towards green products available in the market and to evaluate their future buying intention of green products.

The study has been conducted in two stages. In the first stage, large number of literature reviews were collected and assessed. This stage of the research is quite quantitative in nature. Followed by the second phase of data collection which was mostly based on qualitative techniques i.e. in-depth interviews were conducted among the sample respondents with the support of a well-structured questionnaire to examine the hypotheses of the study.

The researcher applied two different types of sampling techniques for the effective conduct of this study. To identify and define the geographical region the researcher adopted cluster-based random sampling and for the collection of primary data from the sample respondents the researcher adopted convenient sampling technique. The total population of this district is

2916620. Out of 930882 population size 477937 males and 452945 females are residing in the city.

The entire Coimbatore city is geographically divided into five regions: East, West, North, South and Center. Each region is subdivided into 20 wards constituting a total of 100 wards. A sample of twenty-five per cent i.e. 25 wards were chosen as sample. From each region (North, South, East, West and Center) of the city five wards were selected for field survey. Since the researcher encountered practical difficulties in approaching all consumers residing in the selected wards, a sample of 30 respondents from each ward was chosen for the study which made 150 respondents in each region that made up a total sample size of 750 respondents from five regions of Coimbatore city.

5.2.   Findings of the Study

Major findings of the study are briefly summarized in this sub-section.

5.2.1   Demographic and Socio-Economic Status of the Consumers

- The demographic characteristics of the respondents indicated that majority (54.93 per cent) of the respondents are females and 29.07 per cent of the respondents are in the age group of 25-30 years. It has been concluded that 30.80 per cent of the respondents have completed UG degree.

- The studies found that majority (78.40 per cent) of the respondents are married. Further, it has been observed that 24.80 per cent of the respondents are self- employed entrepreneurs.

- It is evident from the detailed data analysis that the consumers in the income bracket of ₹.10001- ₹.40000 prefer buying green products and further, it has been clearly inferred that 52.27 per cent of the respondents live in nuclear family set-up.

- It has been evidenced from the study that 44.40 per cent the respondents have four members in their family. The study found that 51.47 per cent of the respondents surveyed belong to dual income family category.

5.2.2   Consumers' Awareness about Green Products

- The study concluded that 36 per cent of the respondents have moderate level of awareness towards green products.

- The results of One-Way ANOVA test exhibit that there exists a close association between consumers' level of awareness towards green products and their demographic and socio-economic status.

- The study found that 97.73 per cent of the respondents have sourced information about green products from yoga class, art of living class, seminars, public gathering and from other naturopathy classes etc.
- The study observed that 77.73 per cent of the respondents have said that they identify the green products through the natural ingredients used in manufacturing the products like cosmetics, home cleaning products, disinfectants, packing materials etc.
- The results of chi-square test revealed that consumers' level of awareness towards green products helps in recognising products as green or not.

5.2.3   Consumers' Attitude towards Green Products

- The study found that 84.40 per cent of the respondents (mean score of 4.22) believe that green products are better than non-conventional products.
- The study found that majority (79.40 per cent) (mean score of 3.97) of the consumers pay attention to the advertisement claim made about the products and try to frame an attitude towards the products.
- The results of multiple regression exhibited that consumers' level of awareness towards green products is influenced by their level of attitude towards it.

5.2.4   Consumers Buying Behaviour towards Green Products

- The study revealed that majority of (40.80 per cent) of the respondents have said that they always prefer buying green products.
- The study found that 36.40 per cent of the respondents have said that the friends and colleagues mostly influenced their perception towards green products and their values and it has been found that 58.93 per cent of the respondents have been consuming green products for the past 1-3 years.
- The study observed that majority (75.73 per cent) of the respondents prefer to buy wooden products.
- It has been inferred that 65.31 per cent (8.49 mean score) of the respondents have said that long usage of organic products in the family greatly influenced their adoption towards green products.
- The results of Kendall's co-efficient of concordance confirmed that the factors that influence consumers to buy green products differ from one individual to another.

5.2.5   Consumers Level of Perception and Satisfaction towards Green Products

- The study findings indicated that majority (mean score of 4.35) of the respondents believe that green products are healthier and safer.

- The results of multiple regression exhibited that the consumers' level of attitude towards green products is influenced by their level of perceptions towards it.

- The study found that majority (81.80 per cent) of the consumers (mean of 4.09 on the Likert's five-point scale) have exhibited high degree of satisfaction towards the green products available in the market.

- The results of multiple regression exhibit that there exists a close association between consumers' level of perception towards green products and level of satisfaction towards it.

5.2.6   Consumers' Belief on Benefits of Buying Green Products

- The study inferred that consumers have been benefited from having a healthy home and family and conversion to health life-styles, due to consumption of green products.

- The results of One-Way ANOVA test indicated that consumers' level of agreeability about benefits obtained by buying green products varies among their demographic and socio–economic status.

5.2.7   Problems Faced by the Consumers' while Buying Green Products

- It has been concluded that majority (51.20 per cent) of the respondents have said that they have faced problems while buying green products.

- The study found that majority (72.50 per cent) (mean score 7.25) of the consumers fear buying green products due to various reasons like fear of malpractices, lack of trust, past bad experiences etc.

- The results of independent z-test indicated that the consumer faces fewer problems while buying green products in comparison to non-conventional product consumers.

5.2.8   Consumers' Intention towards Future Buying of Green products

- The study observed that 60.80 per cent respondents have said that they surely prefer buying green products in future.

- The results of multiple regression confirmed that consumers' level of satisfaction towards green products influences their preference of continuing to buy green products in future.

- The study found that 59.47 per cent of the respondents have been using green products instead of non-conventional products.

- The study concluded that majority on an average of 97.98 per cent of the respondents prefer using green products for the following reason: Changing people's attitude towards usage of traditional products.

- On an average of 98.68per cent of the respondents are not using green products as these products are not well promoted by Government of India.

5.3. Suggestions

Based on the study findings the following suggestions are proposed to the manufactures, marketers in particular and consumers in general. Greening the products is also not a single step process. Companies have to move towards green gradually, adopting green manufacturing, green product, and green communication and so on. A few suggestions proposed to the green product manufacturers and marketers are summarised in this section of the study:

5.3.1. *Increasing Awareness on Green Products*

The study found that 97.73 per cent of the respondents have sourced information about green products from yoga classes, art of living classes, seminars, public gathering and from other naturopathy classes etc. This indicated that marketers or manufactures take least measure in promotion on benefits and product categories of green products. Thus, the following suggestions are given to them.

- The marketers and manufacturers should increase their promotional activities and publish more advertisements on the green products.
- Since, the study has found that majority (79.40 per cent) (mean score of 3.97) of the consumers pay attention to the advertisement claim made about the products and try to frame an attitude towards the product, the advertisements and promotional campaigns should also focus to make popular about their brands and products categories.
- The study found that only 40.80 per cent of the respondents have said that they always prefer buying green products. By enhancing advertisement and promotional activities the marketers and manufacturers of green products can easily convert non-users or non-consumers of green products into active users or consumers of green products.

5.3.2. *Exhibiting Fair and Genuine Marketing Practices*

The study found that majority (72.50 per cent) (mean score 7.25) of the consumers fear buying green products due to various reasons like fear of malpractices, lack of trust, past bad experiences etc. Thus, the marketers are suggested to practice fairness in their marketing practices.

- The marketers are suggested to understand that fact that today's consumers are becoming more and more conscious about the environment protection and they are also becoming socially responsible. Therefore, manufacturers of green products have to react responsibly to consumers' sentiments and their aspirations of consuming environmentally less damaging or neutral products.

- The manufacturers of green products should not deceive their customers by selling non-conventional or less conventional products with the claim of green products. They have to abide by genuine marketing practices.

- Marketers and manufacturers have to strictly adhere to fairness in following green marketing psychology of "Reduce, Reuse and Recycle"-reducing the environmental deterioration and energy consumption, increasing the repeated use of a product and recycling the product for the development of a new product.

- Manufacturers and marketers of green products should try to earn consumers' confidence by clearly specifying their product manufacturing process, ingredients or products used in manufacturing products on the label or package of the products.

5.3.3. Increase the Frequency of Buying Green Products

The study observed that majority of the sample population does not buy green products on regular bases. The manufacturers and marketers of green products should encourage their customers to buy green products on regular bases.

- For encouraging the customers for purchase of green products the manufacturers and marketers of these products have to create a continuous awareness about the benefits of green products among the consumers, and

- They should aim for price reduction or price modification of practices to attract more customers to buy green products.

- Manufacturers and marketers of green products should ensure that more and more varieties of green products are easily available in most of the retail stores or in the product-specific stores and there should be uninterrupted supply of these products.

- Green product manufacturers have to ensure that quality products or product of same quality is supplied to consumers during each purchase.

5.3.4. Adhering to Innovation and Modernisation in Green Products

Today, consumers live in the age of modernisation and innovations. They seek innovation and new changes in every walk of their life process.

- In order to attract these categories of customers manufacturers of green products should always aim to introduce innovative and periodically adoptable green products, which could be more user-friendly from consumers' point of view.

- Similarly, it is suggested to the manufactures to encourage the customers to reuse the green products they buy.
- The manufactures should educate consumers about the benefits of reusing the green products once bought.

5.3.5. *Focus on More Promotions and Offers*

The study found that 67.76 per cents of the respondents had opined that "poor promotions and offers" is one of the reasons for poor consumption of green products. Thus, marketers are suggested to increase the offers and promotional practices for strengthening their green product sales.

5.3.6. *Pay Attention to the Product Package and Labelling*

The study observed that the sample population pays least attention in checking nature of ingredients used in the product manufacturing /process and the product packages design (like paper, tetra packages, recyclable plastics, natural products, glass etc.). These two mistakes made by the consumers can support the manufactures and marketers to easily cheat their customers.

- Thus, the manufacturers and marketers of green products should encourage their consumers to check these features, whenever they buy green products.
- They should encourage their consumers to understand that fact that by checking the green products labelling actively the consumers can ensure the sustainability of mother earth.

5.4. Conclusion

Green marketing is one of the major trends in modern business. It is used to satisfy the consumers' wants needs, to protect the environment and benefit the society in a more environmentally friendly way. Green marketing thrives on the underlying philosophy "Reduce, Reuse and Recycle". Marketers today use myriads of terms to convey the green value of their products and services and they use "green" as an umbrella term to define anything that is natural, recyclable and not detrimental to the environment and the earth. Consumers' spending patterns and also the demand for green products have been growing rapidly over the past few decades. They have also developed a curiosity to understand how green a green product is.

The study concluded by stating that human wants are unlimited but resources are limited on the earth. So it is essential for the companies to fully utilise the resources without waste or with minimum possible waste. It is also important to achieve organizational profitability. So the marketers cannot ignore green marketing. Consumers' interest is increasing day by day in environmental protection. They are changing their attitude and buying behaviour due to environmental awareness. Need of green products and services have been felt by consumers all over the world. In short, green marketing provides many benefits and has huge growth possibilities for marketers, and manufactures.

5.5.   Future Scope of the Study

Based on the limitations of the study, it has been understood that the survey was limited to Coimbatore city only. Therefore, there is a future scope for the extension of study to the other geographical regions. Even inter-state comparison of consumers' attitude, preferences and buying behaviour practices of green products can be carried out. The future studies can be conducted in analysing

- Consumers' attitude, preferences and buying behaviour practices of green products in various cities of Tamil Nadu like Coimbatore, Trichy and Madurai.
- Comparison of consumers' attitude, preferences and buying behaviour practices of green products in the five Southern States.
- Comparison of consumers' attitude, preferences and buying behaviour practices of green products in various cities of Tamil Nadu like Coimbatore, Trichy and Madurai.

References

[1] T.A. Saleena, "SWOT Analysis of Green Marketing in India", EPRA International Journal of Economic and Business Review, Vol. 3, No. 12, 2015.

[2] Pusarla Lakshmi Padmaja and Vaddadi Krishna Mohan, "A Study on Consumer Perspective towards Green Products in Bengaluru City, India", Journal of Economics and Business Research, Journal of Economics and Business Research, Vol. 1, Pp. 137-151, 2016.